AN EYE ON
THE HEBRIDES

CROIG
MULL

MRS. Galbraith's
Honesty Box

for John — who wanted to know more about the Islands

LEWIS

Oct. 22
Port of Ness

Boats pulled
up for the
winter

Gugas (gannets)

Calum described it, no self respecting chicken would complain o'er long at the method of killing. Conservationists cannot all be vegetarians, surely? During the Second World War when nobody went to Sula Sgeir, the numbers of gannets went *down*.

In 1981 the Wildlife and Countryside Commission Bill inserted an EEC originated clause allowing the tradition to go on, providing only ten men take no more than 2000 birds. Only on Sula Sgeir is this allowed.

The 'Ten Men of Ness' are fiercely proud of retaining the traditional methods and rituals of the Guga Hunt as Calum's wadge of photographs of this year's 'hunt' showed.

At the start of the trip, six months previously, St Kilda had been a symbol of intangibility and all that was ultimate in Hebridean dream islands. As the months passed, its reality was experienced and rationalized. Here at the north of Lewis, as I was about to close the sketchbooks and notebooks, it was still laying claim to my consciousness.

Which island did I like best?

There is no particular one. The perfect island is an amalgam of them all, I suppose. Or where the heart is.

All I know is that I do not know which is worse: being left on the pier or going away on the boat . . .

AN EYE ON THE HEBRIDES

An Illustrated Journey
by
MAIRI HEDDERWICK

CANONGATE

The Gaels have a wonderfully ambivalent proverb that absolves them
of responsibility for the absolute truth of any given piece of
information:

   'Ma's briag bhuam e, is briag h-ugam e'
   (If it be a lie from me, it's a lie to me)

Population statistics that appear in the book are based on the 1981
census.

The publishers would particularly like to thank The Scottish Post
Office Board for believing in this island odyssey from the outset and
for providing financial assistance.
   Such sponsorship is particularly appropriate when we consider the
crucial role the Post Office plays in the lives of the islanders. Not
only are letters and parcels delivered to the most remote crofts and
passengers carried on the postbus, but the Post Office is itself often
the focal point for activity, particularly on the smaller islands.
   The author would like to thank Caledonian MacBrayne whose advice
and route planning kept the van steering in the right direction.

First published in Great Britain in 1989 by
Canongate Publishing Limited.
Paperback edition published in 1991, reprinted in 1992 and 1994 by
Canongate Press Ltd, 14 Frederick Street, Edinburgh

Text and Illustrations © Mairi Crawford Hedderwick 1989

Design by Ann Ross Paterson

British Library Cataloguing in Publication Data
A catalogue record for this book is available on request from the
British Library

ISBN 0-86241-348-6

Typesetting and composition by C. R. Barber, Fort William.
Printed and bound by Butler & Tanner Ltd, Frome.

CONTENTS

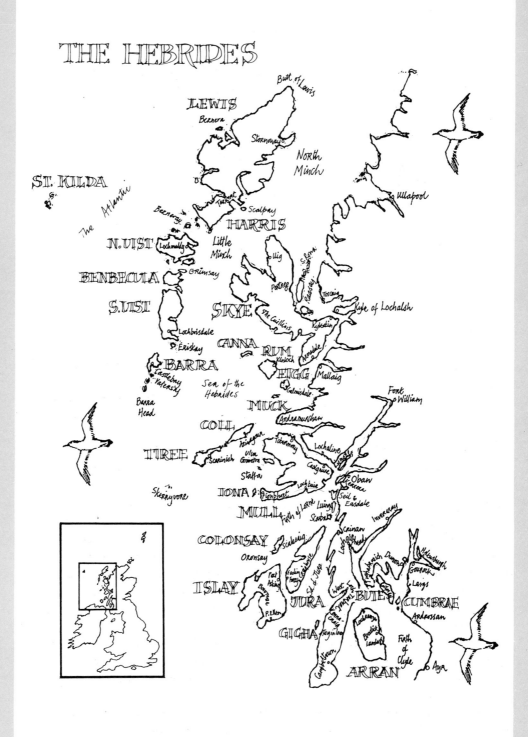

THE HEBRIDES

Approaching Staffa.
Davy Kilpatrick at the helm

Introduction

Most people dream of being in a position to take six months 'out'. Alone. And to the location of their dreams . . .

To be able to justify and implement this selfish fantasy is indeed an enviable situation to be in. I set off to do just that in a doughty old camper van, gearless bicycle atop.

Travelling alone offers total freedom of choice on timetabling and route planning. It also offers the private cop-out clause with impunity. Months of planning and several days of second thoughts had gone into the project: to continuously travel and sketch throughout the length of the Hebrides.

Since childhood, the islands of the West coast have had an extraordinarily powerful effect on me. Our house in Gourock, high on the hill, overlooked the River Clyde. I soon learned to tell the time of day by the different boats that steamed or paddled their way southwards and westwards along the Clyde Coast, some eventually going to the distant Atlantic. The destination names of the mailboat *Lochfyne* and the cargo boat *Loch Carron* were sweet music to my young ears; Colonsay, Iona, Coll, Tiree, The Uists, Harris and Skye.

In those days all these islands were supplied from the waterway of the Clyde. As I got older I realised with shameful awareness that being born on the south side of the river meant that I was an inferior being. I was a Lowlander. I wanted to be a Highlander and Islander.

My first island was Arran. School holidays were spent there with three aged spinster aunts, the Miss Crawfords of Chestnut Cottage in Corrie. Here I heard Gaelic spoken for the first time. The eldest—and biggest—Aunt Jean, uprightly stiff with rheumatism and stays, told many tales of derring-do in her father's skiff in which she regularly rowed out to meet the packetboat from Ayr. I thought she was wonderful. As was her island, her way of talking, her girdle scones so thick and salty compared to the perjinck versions of Tower Drive, Gourock.

Student jobs on the islands of Arran and Coll and ten years of family rearing, 60's style, on Coll was the culmination of that childhood dream. Subsequent years of mainland exile were made tolerable by recidivist return.

Hence the decision to 'do' the Hebrides in an attempt to come to terms with this island obsession.

The journey was continuous and encompassed 40 islands, 750 sea miles, 4,500 land miles, 30 boats, innumerable breakdowns—mechanical and spiritual, including two overnight punctures in magnificent but remote locations; to say nothing of the four very big storms (Cumbrae, Muck, Harris and St Kilda) and the barely-contained sea sickness; the sunstroke (Mull, Barra); the millions of midges the size of eagles (Rum); the far too many soul-searing sunsets.

And every day for 195 days the discipline of sketching, sometimes five or six times a day. I had bargained for the midges and the sea sickness but not for the exhaustion caused by such an intensive daily activity. The self imposed regime was hard; alleviated, however by the many bemused islanders who befriended me along the way and island friends who provided me with baths and meals and beds when the going got rough. Not only did I have an eye on the Hebrides, I was privileged to have an ear on them as well, listening and talking as much as drawing and painting.

The moods of the islands change as quickly as those of the traveller. Sun, rain, wind or midges can be the chief memory of a particular place. On reflection one wonders what these journeys are for? To discover ourselves or our surroundings? By the end of my journey I think that I found the answer.

Like the islands themselves the answer is elusive and, at heart, private. It is several years, the late '80s, since the 'momentous' journey. A time of accelerating change, especially in communications, that still shifts and shunts the island communities ever forward to the new millenium. Never before have the old ways been under such threat. There is a generation of old people on the islands that will take something with them when they go that cannot be replaced. At least two of the old characters I met are no more.

The new ways, unsettling though they are, will surely have their own integrity given time.

Since the first publication of this book Gigha has had three different owners, Muck its first pier, Vatersay is causeway-linked to Barra and most of the Rare Breeds have left Coll. Conservationists and superquarriers battle over the ancient rock of Harris. Traditional jobs in farming and fishing diminish as employment in tourism expands. Islay has a swimming pool.

But some things never change. The sunsets, the storms. And the sea that surrounds us all. 'The water in between' always has the final say in the making of our individuality.

Mairi Crawford Hedderwick
Isle of Coll 1994

· Lochranza ·

Arran, *Arainn, March 19*

approx population: 4,500
Land area: 166 sq. miles

I arrived in Arran on a damp mid-March morning. Brodick pier was quickly deserted after the boat had gone back to the mainland. There is nothing more silent than an island pier after the boat has called. Where does everyone go to?

Notice: Ribbeck's Garage · BRODICK

Arran has a large resident population which almost trebles once the tourist season gets under way. The invading hordes had not yet turned up.

Hotels and boarding houses were dead-eyed save one with open doors. It was cluttered up with 4 by 2 timbers. The owner, clad in a leather apron with a pencil

9

Brodick. Arran.

New snow on the Fell & the Beach Huts wondering if they'll "do" another Summer

behind his ear, was preparing to extend his property and, perhaps, the season. Only another fortnight and it would be Easter. Till then a single blue-hulled catamaran was moored on the gently rain-pocked bay. Rows of empty pink floats bobbed in languid limbo.

Leaving behind the slowly emerging chrysalis of the capital, I headed north to Corrie, ancestral home of one set of forbears. There had lived the 'Old Aunties'. The Misses Jean, Bessie and Nellie Crawford. All dead now, but the village looked the exact same. I felt safe the first night in the van knowing full well that the kind bossy eye of Big Aunt Jean was on me.

The next day—day one of 195 days—was sparkly with a hint of frost. The Firth of Clyde was a band of creamy blue silk below an even bluer sky. There was new snow on Goatfell. I washed bravely in the burn, returning to an open-door breakfast in the van. Little unbroken incoming waves lapped at the edge of my foreshore patio.

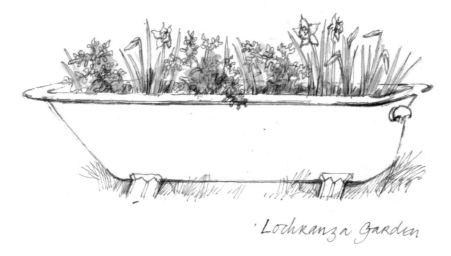

'Lochranza Garden

A porpoise rhythmically undulated a perimeter patrol of our adjoining policies. Little flies shimmered above the gorse in full bloom.

What a euphoric beginning for the van and I.

Arran was one of the first of the islands in the '60s to develop the symbiotic link with growing numbers of summer visitors and the new wave of mainland invaders, called artists and craftspeople.

Invaders, white settlers, green settlers, refugees, ferry loupers—different islands, different names. On Arran at the beginning of this century, they were called KERRSAGINS meaning 'the Kerrs—again' referring to the predominant family name of Irish settlers. Today they could be called YORKSAGINS. Cheery Yorkshire accents abound behind counters and on village hall platforms.

There always have been 'invaders' and always will be. It is a vexed question. I was to meet it time and again in the months ahead.

I set out to climb Goatfell with one of those early artistic settlers. Steve had also been a founder member of the Arran Mountain Rescue, which was reassuring when high winds turned us back at the snow-covered col.

Determined to climb to the top of my first island peak and set a standard for the rest of the trip, I set off on my own next day blessed with sun and little wind. Ice-coated snow and no crampons on the last pitch reminded me that killer mountains do not have to be Munros. Descending geology students—'the Geolly Boys' —whooped their fleet-footed achievement back down the length of the Corrie burn.

There is another Arran on the opposite side to the limbering up hoteliers and traders. 'Try our Candy Floss. The only machine on Arran' already proclaimed Joe's Newsagents in Whiting Bay.

The Geolly Boys. Corrie. Early Morning

Catacol Pub
Two members of the local
band returned from rehearsal,
disconsolate. The accordionist
has tennis elbow.
Watch Video of the Big Fight instead.

"When gorse is out of bloom kissing's
out of fashion"

IN MEMORY OF
SHEENA
DECEMBER 1956 ~ NOVEMBER 1978

Sheena's Seat.
·Sannox·
One of the many dedicated seats to be found in sites of restful beauty all over Arran

IN LOVING MEMORY
OF
EDWIN R. ROSE
WHO DIED ON GOATFELL
15 JULY 1889

Over to the south and west are the rolling fields and long standing hedgerows of Sliddery and Machrie. Budding daffodils speared through last year's dead grass. Lamb gangs played King of the Castle on an upturned trough. Their mothers grazed seriously on.

Parked that night by Kildonan shore, I enjoyed a *son et lumière* performance as the Pladda Lighthouse beamed into the darkened van. A dramatic Beethoven piano concerto on the radio accompanied the simmering tatties—Arran Wonders, of course—and wild chive leaves picked in Glen Ashdale.

The following morning the Geolly Boys—and a jolly girl or two—passed by on an early trudge to find rock samples. The previous night's bar smoke from the Kildonan Hotel still thickly woven into their jackets.

To the north and west of Arran, wild coastline and moors with the place names South, Mid and North Thundergay lead to eerie cliffs near Lochranza where an all year round sunless spot is recorded in the Guinness Book of Records. Thousands of red deer know this is silent country, free of transistors—and candy floss.

The latest edition of *The Arran Banner* had just been published before I boarded the boat for the return to Ardrossan. 97% of the population of the island take the once weekly newspaper. The back page is crammed with 'What's On' diary dates. From brass bands to sub aqua, (do these two ever get together?) it is exhausting enough activity to just read through the list of clubs and events.

I noted that the clocks were to be put forward that weekend and that the opening of the Lochranza Tennis Club was scheduled for 3.00 p.m. on Saturday.

Unfortunately I would be unable to attend. There were thirty nine more islands to visit.

Cumbrae, *Cumaradh, March 29*

approx population: 1,611
Land area: 9 sq. miles (including Little Cumbrae)
'Due to adverse weather conditions at Ardrossan Harbour the *Isle of Arran* will be diverting to Gourock.' I needed to get to Largs, northwards of Ardrossan, the scheduled port, for the crossing to Cumbrae. Huge grey, spray-frayed waves, looking as ludicrously artificial as the wind tunnelled ones in Atlantic Convoy film sets, raced the car ferry northwards up the Clyde. Arran, and soon Cumbrae and Bute, were left behind in a furious salty haze.

Cumbrae Ferry

Gray Day Cumbrae

The robotic intrusion of Ravenscraig ore terminal at the first corner.

Armed for most eventualities, especially the sea in its rougher moods, I sucked some homoeopathic travel pills, adjusted my Chinese pressure point wrist bands, took alternate nibbles of brown bread and apple (Icelandic fisherman's tip) between sips of brandy (my tip), and arrived in Gourock in fine fettle for the immediate return land journey. Back along the self-same shore edge to rain-lashed Largs.

The afternoon ferries to Cumbrae had been cancelled but there were firm assurances that the tea time boats for the high school children and the islanders would be sailing. Too early in the season to be worrying about holiday folk. Hot apple strudel and real Italian icecream in '30s luxury liner style Nardini's, pleasantly stabilised the heaving world and passed the wild weathered time.

Cumbrae was 'discovered', before the Isle of Bute, by Glaswegian Victorian holiday makers. Reflecting initial discretion, Millport's promenade architecture is more restrained than that of Bute's capital, Rothesay, which became *the* heyday seaside resort of its time. Thirty odd steamer sailings a day, with accordian and brass bands on deck, paddled to and fro the islands of the Clyde. Now a five minute car ferry takes the Cumbrae passengers and supplies to the new concrete slipway. Everyone is encapsulated in individual cars and lorries and vans, locked into their own dashboard music or Scottish central belt road reports depending on the direction of travel.

The majority of people living on Cumbrae commute to work on the mainland. Some as far as Glasgow. The population is almost exclusively domiciled in Millport. There is not much else to Cumbrae but a circular ten mile road coasting between the sand and rock foreshore and grazing farm land.

There are no arty colonies on this faded little island. A few solitary artists enjoy its ambivalent singularity. One is a *local* . . .

THE OLD
PIER LIGHT

"The Riding School"
going along the
seafront
MILLPORT

Flounders. 2 eyes on Egyptian profile.
There are left faced eyed & Right faced eyed flat fish.

Giant Fat
Starfish

— like overweight
Pierrots sticking
pudgy fingers
in naughty
places

DAHLIA SEA ANEMONES

With good feeding a lobster will shed
its skin twice yearly. This one needs a
change of diet?

Marine Laboratory
Millport

'Honest to goodness, straightforward jobs are what this place needs', said the tractor man, cutting the first promenade grass of the year. 'Millport Pier was closed down 2 years ago. It was the death of the island'. He will be all right, cutting the grass once a week from now on for the duration of the summer; as will his dog, cocking its leg on the railings above the pink sands of Kames Bay. But there is hope that the pier will be re-opened.

Within twenty four hours the storm had given way to shirtsleeve days and freezing nights. One clear frosty night was spent at the highest point, all of 415 feet, where the one other main road winds inward and upward. Standing on the top of Cumbrae by the Glaid Stane you can look round the island perimeter quicker than you can swing the proverbial cat. That high night, the starlit skies were like a planetarium. As with the storm waves, the manmade likeness is easier to describe than the reality. The carousel lights of mainland and sky pivotted around the van and the Glaid Stane; the stars above, delicately sharp and coolly superior to the ice-lolly orange lights on land. All were trembling save the slow syncopated flashes of lighthouses and mid-channel beacons. Far to the east over the Ayrshire hills lay the false dawn glow of inland urbanity, to the west the black velvet silhouette of Bute.

Such perfection to a day's ending must be shared, if not with a person, at least with one's stomach. We had fresh billy can baked mackerel presented by the Marine Laboratory, one of the few research centres in Britain that supplies sea creatures for academic study. To how many did I deny their supper that night? And garlic leaf salad, from the grounds of the smallest collegiate cathedral in Britain. The leaves were blessedly sweet.

In the morning all those twinkling prettinesses were gone. On the mainland the mothballed oil-fired station at Inverkip, the giant robotic cranes of the ore terminal for Ravenscraig and the cement-grey blocks of visual blight that are Hunterston were all too uncomfortably close.

As if to further mock tiny Cumbrae—a child's ideal of an island,—a half submerged nuclear submarine slunk darkly and stealthily past Fintry Bay.

A young Sculptor in Residence at the Marine Laboratory said she liked the duality of living in such a beautiful place so close to such ugliness.

It is one way of looking at the view.

Bute, *Bòd, March 31*

approx population: 6,800

Land area: 47 sq. miles

Farm lorry. at Wemyss Bay waiting for ferry to Bute.

Livestock and feed lorries always seem to be waiting in the queue at Wemyss Bay for the ferry to Rothesay on the Isle of Bute. Like Cumbrae, Bute is owned by Lord Bute and of the eighty odd farms, all with the exact same plum-coloured entrance signs, only four or five are not leased from His Lordship. Prime farming country quietly rolls and stretches behind and beyond the seaside resort facade of Bute.

Picture window 'improvement' is not allowed in any of the traditional properties

owned by the Marquis. Planning permission is only given to modern houses that have astrigals on the larger-by-law windows, whether structural or not. An aesthetic dictatorship that some island Councils should consider before the uniformity of the assembly line kit house dominates the wilder reaches of our landscape.

The Victorian promenade frontage of the main town, Rothesay, is the home of legendary dragon landladies and convivial pubs. I had to sample one of each. The boarding house primarily for a bath, the pub for another kind of immersion. Both were delightful architectural confections of turn-of-the-century excess with flutings and columns and curlicues, modern pastel painted, the first giving the impression of walking into a many tiered christening cake. The music for 'Annie Laurie' sat stiffly on the piano in the lounge. The landlady was no dragon, only somewhat secretive as to the whereabouts of the bath plug that I had failed to find in the puce pink bathroom.

Rothesay Bay   Easter Sat.

Easter Sunday. Holy Isle, Arran from St. Blane's, Bute
(long after the dawn has risen.)

'They jiner lads have bath after bath if yi don't watch them', she confided as she unlocked the wall cupboard in the hall and withdrew the plug on a string. 'Just see and bring it back to the kitchen when you're done.' I didn't, thinking of the hapless young joiners and planning a second bath and knicker wash before I left.

The pub was *very* convivial, it being the beginning of Easter weekend. Glasgow voices 'frae up the waater' abounded. But something was missing in the cacophony of liquid amber camaraderie: no swearing. Swear words are *never* allowed in the Golfers' Bar.

Eva, the proprietrix, pulls pints benignly sharp-eared below the ornate altar of her gantry. To sever a Lowland male, holidaying or not, from his favourite adjective, is no mean feat.

At Kilchattan P.O. a sign in the window announced 'Easter Service—6.45 a.m.—St Blane's Chapel'. The 12th century ruins of St Blane's nestle 200 feet high in a half amphitheatre of wooded hills. There is a path up through south facing fields.

In the sharp pre-dawn chill, presaging another day's heatwave, the faithful arrived, muffled and mitted, eggs and hymn books in their pockets. Awakening jackdaws and slamming car doors echoed over the dim sea, Arran peaks sharp white in the distance. Two portly Elders negotiated the portable organ over two 'wicked' gates that divided the shadowy sloping fields.

Our singing voices were thin compared to the sturdy bellow of the little organ perched on the flattest gravestone. The organist must have been the warmest of us all, his mud spattered trousers pedalling away like fury.

22

'Christ is Risen'. We echoed the duffle-coated minister's fervent shout. The sun still had a little bit to climb behind the eastern wooded hill before spilling its golden light on our heads. 'Ach well', said the minister, cheerily, 'we never *ever* get the timing just perfect. The first time was the worst'.

Four years previously when the old tradition was re-instated, the good folk of the parish of Kingarth and Kilchattan, with the enthusiasm inherent in all new beginnings, turned up well in advance of the advertised time of dawn. Torches were needed to guide the organ up the pitch dark path. The whole service was conducted in a dank pre-dawn gloom. It seemed an inordinately long time—an hour in fact—for the first glow of light to fan up behind that eastern hill and gild the silent jackdaws' treetops.

Nobody, in the early days of planning, had noted that Easter weekend that year would be the weekend to change the clocks.

Over the centuries, generations of jackdaws must have watched many strange comings and goings in that gentle hallowed spot—not all of a peaceful nature. Later on, on that hot blue morning I returned to savour the peace on my own. The jackdaws were squabbling furiously over the pillaged remains of the hard boiled eggs that the children had rolled down the hill.

Gigha, *Giogha, April 4*

approx population: 160
Land area: 9 sq. miles

'Is Gigha further north or south than England?' The locals get ready with the annual trick question as the visitor season starts to get under way. With shock one learns that the island is further south in latitude than Berwick-upon-Tweed.

More of a shock to me was the realization that here really was my first 'Hebridean' island. That compilation of sight, sound and smell that not all of the islands off the West coast of Scotland necessarily have. For only certain ingredients make up that distinct distillation.

First of all it has to be April, May or June. Blue sky, blue sea greening into white beaches fringed with black rock breakwaters. Machair and skylarks. The silicate smell of the sand dunes mixed with the sea damp air. Somebody will bottle it one day.

Touring caravans and camper vans are not allowed on Gigha, Colonsay or Iona, even though there is car ferry access. Easdale, Kerrera, Ulva and Gometra, Muck, Eigg, Rum, Canna, have no car ferries so the issue has no debate. On the basis that the van was a mobile studio and part of a work project, I was able to get written permission to take the van to Gigha and Colonsay, providing it was kept in a fixed site.

Tailing prawns
Gigha · South Pier

Seals waiting

The NOSTAW
(owner Watson's name
spelled backwards.)

The Stone of Tarbert or The Druid Stone Gigha

The bicycle came off the roof of the van for the first time, and I was made aware of the sense behind such a policy decision. Gigha is tiny. With the great expansion of car ferry communication in the islands comes the ironic destruction of the very peace and quiet that the discerning tourist is seeking. But who are we, these 'discerning tourists', to deny the islanders the improved transport systems?

It was for me the beginning of an ambivalence towards the van and its intrusion on the landscape that led in the months ahead to lengthy evening searches for hidden sites.

The MacSporrans who run the Post Office, shop, guesthouse and much more —Mr MacSporran can tot up a list of sixteen job titles, from telephone linesman to undertaker—have rows of bicycles awaiting the caring green consumer tourist.

Achmore Gardens at the tail end of the bulbs and the primulas and the beginning of the azaleas and the rhodies was a colourful yet fading memorial to Lord Horlick who employed ten gardeners over fifty years ago. Now there are only three and a student. The new owner has decided not to plant out the vegetable gardens this year.

There have been a couple of other firsts for Gigha recently; the closing of the creamery and the opening of the pump-ashore salmon farm. Department of Health restrictions made the creamery equipment obsolete. It is seemingly more cost effective to spend millions on the new fish farm.

The last balmy evening I scrabbled up through the tightly bunched and razor-thorned whins of Gigha's highest point to view the sun setting behind the next ports of call—Islay and Jura. Anorak, sketchbook, jam jar and paintbox were casually left at the side of a farm track. It was the last time I was so stupid.

From a height of three hundred and thirty three feet in the fast fading light I turned to see far below a herd of the few remaining Friesian cows on the island slowly plodding their grazing way in line with my belongings. Kamikazi with fear of the sketchbook being cudded with the clover I made a record descent through the lacerating whins.

Did they know there was a sketch of the fish farm inside?

CHURCH of GIGHA
& CARA
Flowering bulbs on
every window

Window in Memory
of JAMES NOCKELLS
HORLICK 1886-1972

Thick perfume of dying hyacinths
Killing me sweetly as I work.

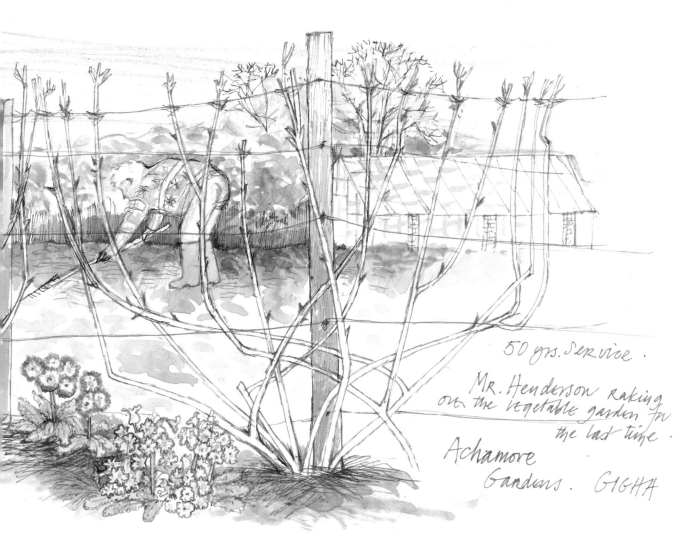

50 yrs. Service.

Mr. Henderson raking out the vegetable garden for the last time.

Achamore Gardens. GIGHA

Islay, *Ile, April 6*

approx population: 3,997
Land area: 401 sq. miles

Islay is big. How can one possibly 'do' islands the size of Islay in one week? That was the allocation if I was to cover forty islands within six months.

Always on arriving on an island I would make for a remote bolthole, after visiting the Tourist Office where possible and grabbing all the local literature. A whisky at the end of the evening chores clarified research and route planning.

Islay Tourist Office is in the new 'square' created by the demolition of some of old Bowmore. The youth of Bowmore skateboarded and ghetto-blasted outside. As yet the Tourist Office has not decided to play Alexander Brothers tapes in opposition. The time might come.

The crazy spring heatwave was cooling. Biting winds blew from the north; fingerless mitts were essential working gear.

But it is very easy to get warm on Islay. There are several distilleries to visit. I did, in between cold forays into geese country and the top of Beinn Bheigeir. There, the hammer-hard wind battered its gusts in one ear and out the other, numbing the teeth in between. That particularly cold day I met an agricultural student with frozen bloody fingers. He had been trying to lift beet; the shaws eaten off by the geese.

The story of the geese of Islay is a classic 'Catch 22' situation. Improved grassland farming methods on Islay, dependent on artificial fertilisers, have attracted the Barnacle geese, especially, from less intensively farmed neighbouring islands. Twenty years ago on Coll we could time the arrival of winter with these beautiful birds. On quiet nights we would hear the scissoring of their grazing. Their droppings were considered to be a blessing to the land. Some maintained that the Caolis and Gunna bullocks got the highest prices at the Oban mart because they ate the droppings.

Not all flew off back to Iceland or Greenland in the spring. A few for the pot were fair game.

The R.S.P.B. bought Gruinart estate in an attempt to provide a sanctuary for the birds. But their admirable original policy of organic fertilisation had to give way to the artificial methods of the majority. The geese much preferred the juiciness of nitrated grass and boycotted the Reserve established for their delectation.

By no means all farmers on Islay are given compensation for goose damage. This causes much ill feeling. Geese do not land with the aid of delineated map references. Human goose scarers are employed, their flapping orange flags moving on wave after wave of disturbed birds.

There must be a compromise somewhere. Some say it should still be in the pot.

Portnahaven P.O. & Church.

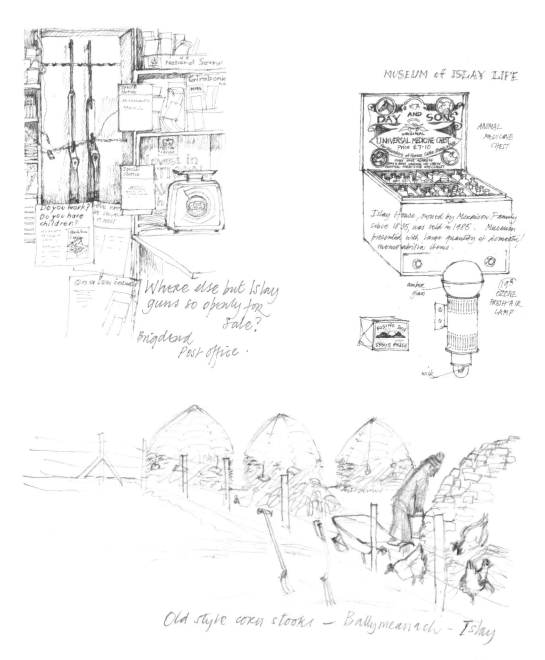

ANIMAL
MEDICINE
CHEST

Islay House, owned by Morrison Family since 1855, was sold in 1985. Museum presented with large quantity of domestic memorabilia items.

amber glass

OZONE
FRESH AIR
LAMP

wick

Where else but Islay guns so openly for sale?

Bridgend,
Post office.

Old style corn stooks — Ballymeanach — Islay

With the vagaries of a planet at climatic war with itself, the latter part of the Islay visit was burnished with brilliant sun. But still that bitter wind. A late night phonecall from the call box above the Cornish style port of Portnahaven was lit by a full frost-ringed moon and the intermittent sweep of the Rhinns of Islay Lighthouse.

Next day I found a boatman willing to take me over to one of the seven remaining manned lighthouses on the West Coast; Ailsa Craig, Pladda, Rhinns of Islay, Skerryvore, Hyskeir (Oban), Butt of Lewis and Cape Wrath. The writing was on the dazzling white walls of the Rhinns however. The three keepers—alternate month on and off—were waiting for the final axe. Computers had already been installed.

Rhinns of Islay
Lighthouse

from deserted (12th) chapel. Soon lighthouse
to be deserted. Computers
already installed

We mused over the previous week's news headlines that told of the electric train that had travelled thirty six miles, unmanned, on the Brighton line and wondered for the automated safety of the seas around our coasts.

A colony of seals sunbathed on the rocks, tail flippers ecstatically arched to the Greek blue sky. Alistair pointed out his pet. Born last September on the lighthouse jetty and subsequently familiar with humans during its land based-puphood, it was very obviously apart from the rest of the clan. 'He's always like that. It is almost as though his mother had rejected him right from the beginning by giving birth on the jetty.'

I had the fanciful notion of a tired, even flippity, young mother seal depositing her burden, calculatedly, hoping for a foundling's future for her unwanted offspring.

I thought Islay was the friendliest place I had yet been to; almost to the point of suspicious effusiveness. Everywhere, but everywhere, people waved as the van and I passed. It was not until leaving I learnt that the lady at the Port Charlotte Museum had the exact same model, colour and year registration of VW caravanette.

How could there possibly be a twin to my old Blue Lady?

We were still in love with each other, the van and me.

Portnahaven . Islay
Mail Time

Jura, *Diùra, April 14*

approx population: 205
Land area: 141 sq. miles

For more than twenty years there has been a campaign lobbying for an overland route to Islay through Jura. A short frequent sea crossing from the mainland to the

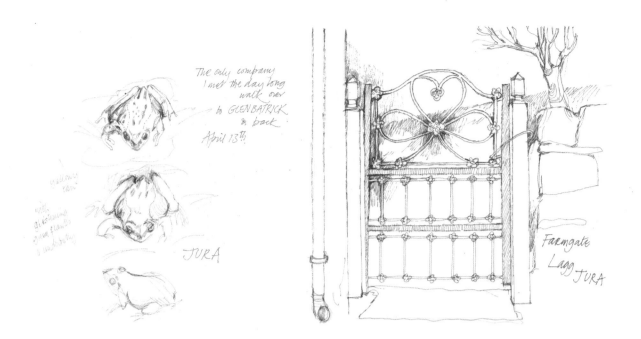

The only company
I met the day long
walk over
to GLENBATRICK
& back
April 13th

JURA

Farmgate
Lagg
JURA

north end of Jura would replace the infrequent two hour crossings from Kennacraig to Port Askaig and Port Ellen in Islay. Weather conditions would not be so adverse in winter, and it would 'open up' Jura. The road in Jura only goes two thirds of the way northwards: thereafter there is a Land Rover track. A costly exercise.

Meanwhile Jura slumbers; a large mysterious giantess, her mountain Paps, on sunny days, coyly capped in misty muslin mutches. The 200-odd inhabitants mostly live in Craighouse; the rest of the island is a wilderness.

I have always found Jura a very strange island. The Paps of Jura are said to be the mythical habitat of women with magical powers. There are folklore tales of the Seven Big Women of Jura and the Witch of Jura. I was determined to conquer the highest Pap in an attempt to dispel my uneasy feelings.

Despite the extremes of temperature experienced on Islay the days were always dry. Not so on Jura. From the day I arrived it rained and rained . . . and rained. On the one day when the cloud was lifted by a brisk wind, the estate upwind from the mountains decided to do extensive muir burning. The Paps were smothered in acrid heather smoke all day long. Whoever these women were I don't think they wanted to be seen.

What with them and the disproportionate fear of the pilgrimage to witness the gaping, sucking hole of the Corrievreckan Whirlpool at the northernmost remotest part of the island, I think I suffered my first crisis of identity on the trip.

And coming hard on its heels, the first experience of abject loneliness.

I also think the bulk buy of vitamin C tablets were unsuccessfully combating a rotten virus that sapped all energy. That was no doubt why I took the van seven miles up the northbound track, punishing her brutally. I stopped at the back of George Orwell's Barnhill hoping for a night's soothing osmosis. The wild Morello cherry trees that he had ordered from the mainland were in full bloom. They turned out to be common or wild garden Gean.

Corrievreckan was a non-event. I must stop watching 'I Know Where I'm Going' when it comes on the tele again. Only certain combinations of tides and winds create the legendary eight and a half knot holocaust plughole.

The rain went on . . . and on . . .

I weakened and booked into The Jura Hotel. It has a very big drying room and lots of hot water. Also a lecherously smiling black labrador.

In the pub I met a man newly resident on the island—'A writer, I think,' said a local later, not without a frown. 'We get lots of them.' On my travels—I had noticed that writers were regarded with suspicion. Illustrators were not.

Michael from the media south had decided to find 'his island' to live in for the second half of his life. He had spent the previous year travelling in the Hebrides looking for the right combination of available property in the right place. The old Post Office at Lagg was now slowly being done up; in between studying the meaning and mysteries of life in the Western Isles.

He had come up with an ingenious idea to treat the malaise of unemployment in the Highlands and Islands. Instead of issuing dole cheques the Government would pay people for their excess home-produced electricity which by statute already they are obliged to do. 'Even give grants to help people set up their own wind or water powered system. Excess supply being sold to the national grid.'

On Jura it might be hard to get the necessary planning permission. The island is divided into five privately owned shooting and fishing estates. Thousands of acres of privately cultivated silence can be intimidating. Jura is today what the whole of the Highlands and Islands could have remained had there been no local development initiative.

I gave the man from the South the address of the Highlands and Islands Development Board. Just in case he wanted to take his idea further.

Barnhill
where George Orwell, dying,
completed '1984'

Gean
Blossom
&
Pheasant Eye
Narcissi from deer shorn
garden

Apr. 17.

Marion's message to ANY coal lorry that might pass. The usual supplier, having failed to deliver.

Seil, *Saoil, April 21*

approx population: 424
Land area: 8 sq. miles

The Isle of Seil is so close to the mainland a pole vaulter could land dry shod on the other side. Not quite so dramatic is the actual access over its eighteenth century hump-back bridge that spans a seaweed fringed moat. In April rare fairy foxgloves cover the ominous cracks that are appearing on this 'Bridge over the Atlantic'.

Bus parties are eager for the dubious delights of the Easdale Arts Centre, which has promoted to the hilt this crossing. Passengers have to dismount on the mainland, walk over, photograph their 6–7 tons of sedentary luxury slowly tilting upwards, over and down the other side of the bridge before re-uniting bums with seats.

While I was sketching, the hotelier adjacent to the bridge showed overt interest, not based on aesthetics. 'Are you from the Planning Department?' There is talk of a new bridge—further away.

Easdale village on the west of Seil takes its name from the tiny island of Easdale, a little further out into the open seas of the Firth of Lorne. Steep landward cliffs behind the village can be safely climbed if one does not follow the paths of the shaggy long-haired goats, to overview the patchwork of tiny white cottages and oblong ponds of deep black water that cover Easdale Island—all of 400 yards square.

CLACHAN
POST OFFICE

Bella Campbell,
Postmistress, has
taken option of
3 days a week
opening from now on!

Her mother started P.O. in 1917.
The best room is the P.O.

Easdale, *Eisdeal*

approx population: 32
Land area: 35 acres

A small motorboat takes the bus parties over to Easdale Island in relays. Slate workers lived and worked here before the freak storm of 1881 when tides and winds combined to wash over the island and flood the open cast mines. No lives were lost but the quarries never operated again.

A lot of the workers' cottages are now very desirable holiday homes. One house, however, is a People's Palace cornucopia of mementoes, photos, records, artifacts, garnered from the slate quarrying days. All due to the enthusiasm of Jean Adams whose quarryman grandfather left the island after the disaster, heading for London to look for work. There she was eventually born. Not all that long ago she came to visit Easdale for the first time. 'I just stayed.'

With 8,000 visitors last year coming to the Museum her Londoner ferryman husband—'I dragged him up here'—must sometimes yearn for his own bridge over the Atlantic.

EASDALE
MUSEUM.

Jean's
grandfather
who was never a
member of the Independent
Order of Rechabites.
"He liked his wee dram too much"......

Luing, *Luinn*

approx population: 162
Land area: 11 sq. miles

A poignant memorial to the era of industrial exploitation is the graveyard in Luing where even the poorest soul had a slate marking the spot of earthly remains. Slate was abundant and easily inscribed.

I love old graveyards. The more amateur the monumental sculptor the more touching; the more pompous the sentiments the more ludicrous; the more foreign the style the more thought-provoking the universality of our mortality.

Luing graveyard has examples of all three. 'Lachlin Mc Lach[n] 1790' is a simple hand-carved slate with 'memento morry' one-winged angel. Alex Campbell's 1829 double-sided pontifications are on a tall stone that is set into the graveyard wall.

The roadside facia arrests like a wayside pulpit 'HALT PASSENGER TAKE HEED . . .' On the other side, inside the graveyard, is listed self-congratulatory paeans with biblical reference: 'marvelous to most that I digged my grave before I died, as Jacob and Joseph of Arimathea'. Ending with 'and I protested that none go in my grave after me if not have the earnest of spirit to be a child of God as I am of election sure'. And, of course, only 'Pure Presbyterian Religion' qualified for that privilege.

Albert Sultcs was drowned in 1936 when the Latvian S.S. *Helena Faulbaum* went aground off Belnahua Island nearby. A communal grave for fourteen of his shipmates is beside the white continental-style stone, complete with porcelain photo erected by his parents. The Latvian caption is awkwardly translated with poetic effect:

WAS STORM-TORE BLOSSOMS,
DESTROYED DREAMS OF HAPPYNES

Island graveyards, inevitably, have a preponderance of sea-claimed deaths, local and foreign.

Nowadays Luing is famed not for slate but gleaming Burgundy red cattle, whose numbers and pedigree dictate no camping lest their gullets are choked with polythene bags or their hooves cut with broken glass. I chose to interpret that the ban only applied to those with canvas shelters but was always nervous of apprehension. Landowners can have terrible tempers.

I found innocent reassurance one day knocking on a door at Blackmill Bay. I asked permission to leave the van nearby whilst I went to Scarba. A very elderly lady answered. Did she mind? She smiled sweetly, 'Oh, not at all, dear. It's not my land. It belongs to the island.'

Scarba was unplanned. The sunstroke weather was continuing and the temptation of 'a day off' on an uninhabited island was irresistible. I found a fisherman willing to take me over and collect me at the end of the day.

"There was not a horse that would ever go by that well once it had had a drink from it. The horses with the milk carts! Ach, you just had to wait & let them have their fill" Reminisced Irene McLachlan.

Tobhar na Camachachd
Well of the Journey.

Well near Cullipool
Luing.

cushions of marsh saxifrage
stellar clumps of primroses.

Uninhabited Scarba, like others of the smaller islands in the Firth of Lorne is used as a base for Adventure Courses. Besides the isolated bothy there is also a beautiful Big House on a plateau above the woods that is rented out in the shooting season. Both buildings were deserted. I had the island to myself, the deer—and my first cuckoo.

Corrievreckan is easy to see from the south top of Scarba, the blue hazed Paps of Jura nakedly mocking me from the south west. Once again the whirlpool only obliged with a frill of frothing wave as it resisted the oily sworls of current forcing their way through the narrows between Scarba and Jura.

John, in his boat the size of a midge, checked creels on the far side. What nonchalant bravery. The monster that lies dormant at the foot of Corrievreckan might yawn hungrily for a midge that very day.

Coming down from the top I was surprised and annoyed to see *OTHER PEOPLE*. As no doubt were they—the owners of Scarba—and Luing. We chatted pleasantly, however. I never mentioned the van.

Kerrera, *Cearrara, April 27*

approx population: 45
Land area: 7.50 sq. miles

Kerrera must be the most immediately remote island of them all.

It is only 5 minutes by open passenger ferry boat from Gallanach, a few miles south of the large town, fishing port and car ferry terminal of Oban, Gateway to the Western Isles.

Once you step off onto the slipway time stops.

Two British Telecom engineers prepared themselves for the rigours of walking round the scattered households (no cars on Kerrera), via the twisting rutted track that loops the southern two thirds of the island. The north end, called locally 'the Free State', is not in the same thrall to Madame McDougall of McDougall who does not believe in anything moving on, except overnight tourists. Hence the charm of the place.

The teacher comes over each day from Oban with the school dinners in a canister. Children run down the brae to meet her. They walk her up to the school high above the Post Office. The school used to be the church.

What deer are to Jura, and cows are to Luing, so sheep are to Kerrera. The all-over green of the humpy bumpy hills was polka dotted with white. Walking along a dusty tree blossomed track with a retired couple on their daily mission to feed the tame greylag geese of absent neighbours, I could have been on Greece. Swap a blossom, a bird or two. The heat, and the glitter of the sea were the same.

The neighbour's house was a creation of zany love. Passion flowers bloomed in a conservatory shelved with fish boxes. Inside, the proud head and horns of Jacob the wild Barra billy goat were nailed to the wall. Long ago, he had come to Kerrera to improve the island stock. His epitaph tacked below said:

In Memory of JACOB, Ancestor of all the Goats and
PRESIDENT OF THE KERRERA BRIDGE CLUB.

IN MEMORY OF
Jacob
Ancestor of all the
goats and
PRESIDENT of the
KERRERA BRIDGE CLUB

Oris aig
THE BARRA BILLY GOAT.
After he died he was burnt
only up to his neck for
natural cleaning of
his skull.

Passion Flowers blooming in
Stook & Rosemary's
CONSERVATOIRE

Bob & Madge over
to feed the
GREYLAG GEESE
& water
the
plants.

At the north end of the island stands the tall Cleopatra's Needle, a memorial to David Hutcheson, progenitor to Caledonian MacBrayne, the major ferry operators on the West Coast. It says:

'Erected by a Grateful Public in memory of DAVID HUTCHESON by whose Energy·and Enterprise the Benefits of Greatly Improved STEAM COMMUNICATION were conferred on the West Highlands and Islands of Scotland. 1883'

The closeness to Oban at this point is not just geographic. There is the incongruous ability to hear in great detail the noisy workings of a town—a century forward in time. Cars and lorries revved, braked and hooted; a diesel train coughed out of the station; the public address system on a Cal Mac ferry loudly detailed safety procedures, obligatory since the Zeebrugge incident.

Down at the south end of the island Kerrera turned its back on the fumes and furore and slipped into a velvety early evening. I could only hear sheep and curlews.

I wonder if the British Telecom men know that the telephone box at the slipway is used as the collecting point for mainland messages? A bottle of whisky from Willie Low's can sit there all weekend, quite safe, till the owner comes to collect.

12 School Dinners Canister

The School on
the hill that
used to be the
church.
KERRERA

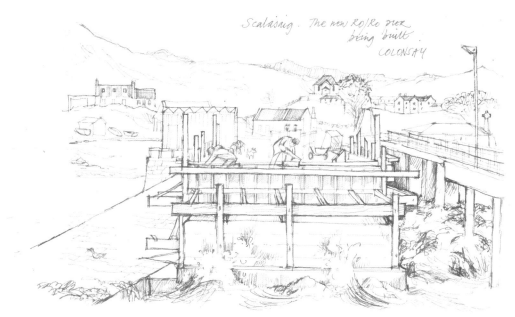

Scalasaig. The new RO/Ro pier
being built.
COLONSAY

Colonsay, *Colbhasa, April 29*

approx population: 13?
Land area: 16 sq. miles

Departure was from that busy Oban pier. In times past, Colonsay has been served from West Loch Tarbert via the Islay run. The folk on Colonsay fought hard to have the link re-established with Oban, primarily for the more direct weekly transportation of secondary pupils to Oban High School. Now Cal Mac propose a shared Oban and Kennacraig timetable consequently making trips to Oban less frequent.

Colonsay has always felt like the geographic pig in the middle in this game of transport economics.

Oronsay is the tidal island attached to the south of Colonsay.

There is a cheeriness and friendliness about Colonsay and Oronsay folk that might well come from the collective spirit created by such battles. On land as well as sea. Somehow one gets the impression of nothing being allowed to get too out of line on Colonsay.

Having arranged special permission to take the van, I miserably prepared myself for the confines of a regimented site. My permanent place was 'anywhere you like', on the deserted south-facing sweep of Machrins Bay.

Hidden behind a rocky outcrop, it was one of the top ten magnificent out-of-sight sites of the trip. At least five of the top ten soul-searching sunsets were witnessed there. Water was from the spring well of Tobhar Fuar gurgling up icy cold a few feet inland from the beach. Watercress sandwiches were always in the bicycle basket.

The van and I had a much needed travelling break from each other. Our relationship had been getting strained. Single handed, I had never been able to lift the extending roof. For six weeks I had stoically accepted hunchback conditions. Our relationship improved a hundredfold on Colonsay, however, thanks to a chance meeting with intelligent friends. With the aid of a 5 ft. baton found washed up on the shore, the ancient principle of leverage enabled me to *stand* to wash, dress and cook from then on.

Carpets of pink purslane, garlic, bluebells, forget-me-nots, aconites & primroses. COLONSAY HOUSE GARDENS.

Horse chestnut leaves just unfolding. Limp & crumpled like the ears of the new born lambs by Loch Fada.

May 1st.

URAGAIG
COLONSAY

I will always associate Colonsay with heightened awareness. And birthday treats . . . dinner, bed and breakfast in the Colonsay Hotel. The menu? Carrot and coriander soup, casseroled guineafowl with ginger sauce, rhubarb fool and shortbread. Wine of course.

Later in the pub in response to the standard tourist query, 'So what happens on Colonsay?' a local replied, 'This is Fantasy Island. Anything *you* want can happen here. Now what would you like?'

More wine . . .

In the morning, the hoteliers Kevin and Christa Byrne were not in a good mood. No boat. Months of negotiations re conditions of service for British seamen had recently been resolved amicably by all except the P. & O. crews. Cal Mac men had come out on a twenty four hour sympathy strike.

Already the phone was ringing cancellations for July and August bookings from the security conscious South. It looked as though the strike might go on. Long stay guests, just arrived on the previous boatday, planned departure on the first available sailing. With only three boats a week to Colonsay they were taking no chances.

Oronsay, *Orasaigh*

approx population: 3
Land area: 3 sq. miles

If no boat comes or no-one on Colonsay has written a first class letter to the one family that lives on Oronsay, then Keith, the Post, cannot offer a lift in the rope festooned Landrover Postbus across the mile strand at low tide. A tourist obliged with a postcard to the McDougall's the day of the strike.

Four and a half year old Mairi McDougall popped out from behind her playground familiars—the gravestones of Oronsay Priory. She offered her self-appointed guideship. Her running commentaries on the fifteenth century stone carved likenesses of Lords and Abbots—and an Abbotess—threw new light on the causes of mediaeval monastic death. 'The monks all died because they were so tired

Sandy's Dad & friend "planting"
trays of oysters (100,000) in Pol Gorm

The Strand   Colonsay / Oronsay

" There is a different kind of person coming on holiday
to the islands nowadays. People who have no understanding
of the sea and its tides, let alone nature in general."

carving the stones all day long. They just lay down on top of the big flat stones—like this.' She demonstrated on top of a table-like tomb with ancient bones at one side gaping through a perspex shield. 'And then, after a while,' she continued, 'they died and went underneath. Would you like to see my baby brother?' All this in one breath. Thank goodness her new baby brother was very much alive and kicking.

There was great excitement in Mairi's home. Her Dad, who manages Oronsay for new American owners, was on the mainland—buying a two-seater hovercraft! This, it was hoped, would enable Mairi to get over the Strand whether the tide was in, out or halfway. She was to start school the next August. The schoolcar would pick her up on the Colonsay side. An ordinary keeled boat at certain tides is unable to float; yet the water is too high for a vehicle to negotiate. Time and tide are not always in agreement when it comes to manmade timetables.

This shallow rise and fall in the tides over miles of sand is just what oysters like. The Abrahams who live at the Colonsay side of the Strand are proving it. Pol Gorm, one of the pools in the Strand, was where Andy with the help of a friend was 'planting' 100,000 young oysters in submersible trays. Whether oysters like hovercrafts or not remains to be seen.

Colonsay Hotel & Church
May 6.

There can be a pleasantly deceptive sense of immediate belonging experienced by visitors to small remote inhabited islands. Locals are quickly identified by their functions and nicknames; if you arrive not too late in the season their enthusiasm for telling tall tales can include you, too. Summer mythmaking is for winter fireside reminiscing. The exploration round this microcosm of society has recognizable limits. As has the physical terrain, both are safely contained by the womb waters of the ocean.

I did not want to leave Colonsay and secretly hoped for the seamen's strike to go on.

Colonsay & Oronsay Post Bus
licensed to carry 4 passengers

Mull, *Muile, May 7*

approx population: 2,365
Land area: 353 sq. miles

As it turned out the seamen's strike facilitated the journey to Mull, my next island, in the most efficient if unscheduled way. Cal Mac ran a mercy trip to Colonsay, but could not guarantee any boats leaving Oban the next day—for Mull or anywhere else. Pickets were arriving from the South.

The Purser, recognizing my dilemma, helpfully put the van on first, into the far recesses of the car deck. As Oban pier is not big enough to accommodate all the Oban-based ferries overnight, the *Columba*, after disembarking all passengers and vehicles there, berths at Craignure on Mull.

Colonsay to Mull by van in one day . . . It must be a record.

Mull, like Islay is big, but higher; Ben More is a Munro. A friend was coming out to witness my sponsored climb for Intermediate Technology. A sensible precaution. My staying power was waning. Three months on the go was beginning to tell.

And the heatwave was at its height. It had not rained since Jura. We did it slowly, embarrassingly so, but, as ever, the view from the top was worth the effort. Mull *is* a big island. And we were on the top of it. Westwards and south, Iona, Staffa, Ulva, Gometra and the Treshnish lay like pewter inlays in a dish of platinum sea.

The van had its first puncture that night. Furious at the machine-compressed tightness of the nuts we had to admit inadequate self-sufficiency and seek help. Knock Farm at the head of Loch na Keal provided the right equipment and brawn . . . and tea . . . and cheese and biscuits . . . and chat.

In the yard of Knock Farm were nigh on fourteen smiling collies lounging about. Every one a past, present or future working dog. Lachie and his two sons need three each at gathering time. 4,000 sheep graze on the very mountain range we had climbed. 'The scree tears the dogs' paws. We have to use them in turns'. Back in the yard the 'oldtimers' tell Top, the pup, son of Roy and Lyn, all about his future. On the tops.

Loch Buie was new country to me. There is a dramatic, dangerous-in-parts, shore walk all the way to Carsaig. Nobody would know for a long time if you had fallen by the tideside. Wild sheep, unclipped for two seasons at least, staggered heavily up into black overhanging cliffs. At the end of the three and a half hour scramble is Inniemore Lodge—and for the cogniscenti the telephone box filmed in 'I Know Where I'm Going' in 1945. It is now dwarfed by forty years growth in the massive pines. The waterfall is the same.

By the time you get to the Ross of Mull the big hills and lonely glens are left behind. Machair swards lead to the sands of Uisken and Fidden (pronounced Feedyin). At the end of the road is Fionnphort, terminus for the Sacred Isle, Iona.

The Tobermory Cherub.
Presented to the Burgh
in 1883 by R. STRATHERN
the mains water supply
contractors.

"The Gallery" Rose Window competing with the tartan
TOBERMORY MULL

Iona, *I Chaluim Chille or I*

approx population: 100
Land area: 4.50 sq. miles

Something sacred to me has to be private and special and immune from interference. In June, Iona was none of these things—save special in the sense of being a magnet attracting hoardes of indiscriminate pilgrims. In busloads.

May. 8.

M.V. MORVEN
Crossing to IONA.

Visitors to Iona.
No·one looking where they are going ··· ···

The Sunday communion service was a bland ecumenical mixture of old and new. Format traditional; vestments contemporary. The altar party of preachers in 'civvie' garb looked so drab against the gold and pink damask embroidered altar cloth with glowing stained glass window behind. Does God really prefer teeshirts below tweed mixture jackets? Training shoes? And a disturbing free-range toddler beyond parental control?

There is a tradition in those cathedral walls that needs to be more formally respected. I'm sure it is. On other occasions.

I ran away from one disappointment to another. The *Iolaire* could not land visitors when we got to Staffa. 'The swell too much and the tide lowering', puffed Davy Kirkpatrick, through his pipe. The disease of litigation will soon produce a nation of impotent voyeurs. We played waltzing games with dolphins on the way back.

Iona must shrink into the inner heart of its being as the season progresses; its outer skin pounded by so many thousands of questing feet. Every knoll and hillock seems to have a cairn atop until one realizes it is an awestruck sightseer.

I hope there is a subterranean tunnel for the spirit of Iona to retreat along—all the way to Ireland maybe—for the summer invasion.

48

Guess which way
the prevailing wind.....

MAOL.   IONA

Hens.
ERRAID

Erraid, *Earraid*

approx population: 6
Land area: 1 sq. mile

Not so far away from Iona are the uninvaded Erraid Isles. A sort of alternative eye
on Iona. Members of the Findhorn Foundation fulfill an islanded realization of
their philosophy.

The Stevenson brothers, of lighthouse fame, used Erraid and Tiree as the
two bases from which isolated Skerryvore lighthouse was built. Stone masons on
Erraid fashioned the stones prior to shipping. Their cottages are lived in with the
distinctive Findhorn label of material ease and responsible organisation. Everything
is very neat, from the rows of vegetables to the rows of communal kitchen utensils
always in the right place; to the neat coils of rope on the jetty and the rings on the
hens' legs aiding accurate culling of old boilers for soup.

Their hospitality shames me to write this. I was feeling very scruffy.

A local woman on Iona said an interesting thing, 'I wonder what it is that
these "alternative" people come here looking for—they all seem such calm,
wonderful, peaceful people anyway. What's lacking?'

The Old
& the New.
STOVES
Lighthouses
ERRAID.

Ulva, *Ulbha*

approx population: 13
Land area: 2 sq. miles

Mull has several inhabited offshore islands. Of these Ulva and Gometra have no albatross of religion or organised tourism round their neck. No cars invade the ambling ambience of an island in aspic. The beech woods in Ulva must be preserved for ever. Fledgling herons swayed high above in the silky soft May green foliage.

Wooden signposts mark the winding ways that start from the ferry shed where a duck called Mr Muscovy roosts with the hens and Buster the cockerel by the fancy new public payphone. The old telephone box outside 'will do fine now for the tomatoes'.

The Ulva primary children go to school on the 'mainland' of Mull, crossing the narrows in the little open ferry boat each day. As does Mr Muscovy. He flies, of course. Just in time for snacks at playtime.

Loch Leader mooring for the night.

Ballachoish GOMETRA. looking on to ULVA.

Mr. Muscovy & the Ulva Payphone

51

Gometra, *Gòmastra*

approx population: 4
Land area: 2 sq. miles

There is a wild barren walk the length of Ulva to the small bridge that connects it to Gometra. Here deer and cashmere goats are being farmed on a gent's handkerchief size of an island, relatively speaking. A sign on a high fence said STAGS CAN BE DANGEROUS.

Beautiful Gometra House, sadly on the teetering brink of deterioration, looks out and over the Treshnish Isles. I had a cup of tea with the island's solitary caretaker. Stags with furry swelling velvet horns grazed on what must have once been the front lawn. They were close enough to take a nibble of our digestive biscuits, if they so wished.

Gometra House & the Dangerous Stags

Cycling back along the bone-shaking track, I was struck by the similarities to Kerrera. A 'Between the Wars' feeling and Brigadoon rolled into one. Through the apple blossom by the deserted houses at Ballacloich I saw the 1892 converted Brixham Trawler *Lorne Leader*, sails stowed, edging her way into the aquamarine creek for overnight anchorage. By 10.30 p.m. it would still be light and I would be back on mainland Mull. Those on board would have explored and possessed 'their' desert island. Save for the caretaker, the goats and the deer, they would believe they had had the sunset all to themselves.

Back in Mull multi-coloured Tobermory was full of townspeople just back from the Glasgow Garden Festival with flower logo-ed carrier bags and car stickers. The Clown Jewels' rainbow-hued Travelling Theatre bus had just arrived in town.

It was parked by the old jetty which was mounded with neon turquoise ropes and sweetie pink floats. Tartan rugs and aprons hung from shop door lintels.

Tobermory was in festive mood. The Burgh's 200th anniversary was being celebrated. Shops were packed with souvenirs. There was also the best range of health and delicatessen goods since Arran.

Once called the Officers' Mess, on account of the high number of ex-army residents, Mull now has the cynical title of Costa Geriatrica. Houses are snapped up by retired people from the South whose property, when sold, finances not only the Highland dream cottage but the car, campervan and boat. All of which sit neatly outside immaculate cottages with landscaped gardens. With judicious investment there is also enough to fund a comfortable little unearned income. Unfortunately this is all at another kind of expense—the less affluent locals who are unable to compete in the house market stakes.

Arran, Mull and Skye all have at least one well stocked wine and fruit and vegetable and delicatessen shop. The Costa Geriatrica does have fruitful rewards. The van headed for the ferry, aromatic with dripping brie, pesto, pine nut kernels and Tobermory trout, smoked with Marjorie Goldie's 'I'm not telling' recipe.

Mull was also memorable for the first midge bite. I'd hoped they had all been killed off by the long-lasting heatwave. Soon it would be earwig time too.

I was nearly half-way through the journey.

Lismore, *Lios Mòr, May 21*

approx population: 105
Land area: 10 sq. miles

More lambs go to market from Lismore (6,400 acres) for the October sales than from the whole of the Isle of Harris (42,000 acres). The island is limestone and chalk based; the fields and meadows lush with pasture. At the roadside, fourteen inch high wild orchids pushed through tangled vetch and clovers, heads the size of golfballs.

Numerous high-banked sideroads go off from the main road that follows the long spine of the island. It is very easy to get disorientated in the hollows of their hillocky ups and downs.

In days gone by, Lismore men were famed for their skills in breaking in carthorses sent from all over the Hebrides. The crumbling jetty over at the old lime quarry at Salen was the sight of many a near-drowning of horse, boat and man. All is now very silent. The great round lime kiln chimneys lined with ivy; workers cottages and stores roofless; the masonry sadly, but gently, blending into the landscape.

The major source of employment in Lismore now, outside of farming, is on the west mainland of Morven at Glensanda, reached by daily speedboat.

There, granite for aggregate is quarried by the millions of tons for export throughout the world. When it is no longer needed the deserted workers' portacabins will have no mellow postlude, as at Salen, for future generations to wander amongst and muse over.

Near drought conditions after almost six weeks sun and wind looked as though they were at last coming to an end. The farmers were pleased. Tourist needs do not count for much on agriculturally prosperous Lismore. Low sulphurous clouds, thick heat and serious spats of heavy rain heralded the break.

The van had its second puncture and its most remote during a 3.00 a.m. precautionary change of stance; a monsoon downpour threatened to moisten the previous evening's rock-hard track to a path of treacle custard.

A sunset site that turned into a sunrise daymare. The midges were in their element.

Lismore and Mull farmers are most obliging.

Roadside
Lismore Orchid
May 21
ACTUAL SIZE
(11" to base)
Early Purple?

Balephuil.

Tiree, *Tiriodh, May 25*

approx population: 780
Land area: 29 sq. miles

After the rains, the storms. The *Columba* turned back before she even got as far as Coll.

I never ever thought I would feel nostalgic about this boat. She replaced a fine old ship, the *Claymore*, on the Coll/Tiree/Colonsay run in 1964. The first 'floating car park and cafeteria' to go to these islands, she was the height of modernity. We all loathed her, yearning for the white tablecloths, steward-served kippers and silver jingling cakestands of the old *Claymore*, now plying the Greek Isles in converted dotage.

The *Columba* was now on her last summer season before being refitted by a private company to cruise the Hebrides, thankfully, instead of the Aegean. Swimming pool on the car deck? Cocktails in the cafeteria?

By now the crew of the *Columba* would cheer when they saw the van appear on the ramp. One bright spark had the temerity to put a 'For Sale' notice secretly on the windscreen in between embarkations. I took it as a lucky omen and hoped that the van was not too depressed. Our relationship had deteriorated again.

Tiree is a living architectural museum of crofthouses, unique to the Hebrides.

MILTON · Tiree
awaiting Tender Loving Care?

THE GREEN.
TIREE

May 29.

Scarinish Secondary School.
Yearly Litter Clean Up   May 30

Balemartin P.O.
Tiree.

Iain's sister, up
from Glasgow to help
with the lambing.

Iain McKinnon
The Hill
Kilmoluaig. Tiree.

Never off the island. Electricity
connection to box outside house. "I
haven't made my mind up yet about
having it inside."

It is not just because of the flatness that they are so arresting, almost seeming to grow up out of the thin line of the land.

Barring the low hills of Ben Haugh, Ben Hynish and the headland of Kenavara, Tiree, they say, is so flat a rabbit and its mate—should they ever be allowed to land—would soon burrow the island under the Atlantic.

Tiree houses can be divided into four categories: thatched, black felters, pudding and plain. Inevitably there is the beginnings of a fifth category, slow to manifest itself on Tiree. The 'kithouse'.

Is it aesthetic, cultural snobbery to decry these new buildings? Why shouldn't people have the latest in contemporary comfort, especially in such windswept climates? For myself, a good draught does no harm and I think you would find thick walls and tiny windows have their own kind of insulation—if lack of space and light.

'Trouble with thatched roofs is—there are a lot of beasties crawling about up there but they don't all end up falling in your soup, as some people imagine', said Frances Walker as she gave me a cup of beastie free tea in her thatched cottage at Ballevullin. She supports the work of Argyll and Bute District Council and the Cairndean nan Taighean Tugha (Friends of the Thatched Houses of Tiree) who work to preserve and modernise internally the still lived-in thatched homes.

May 31 Tiree
1st Real rains for 6 wks
Lambs soaked for first time

57

Kilmoluaig

Vaul

Salum.

Scarinish

TIREE HOUSES
Thatched, Black Felters,
Pudding & Plain.

They are certainly not all the dilettante preserve of holiday owners.

The black felters, the pudding and the plain are evolutions of the thatched house. The 'kithouse' does not quite follow on so smoothly, so organically.

Watching over every house on Tiree is the omnipresent 'golf ball' radar station rising on Ben Hynish like a mad moon.

Tiree is a predominantly crofting island. The Crofter's Commission gives better grants for building new houses than doing up old ones. I hope the Tiristeach are aware of their architectural heritage before it is too late.

Like Tobermory there was a colourful aspect to Tiree. Not in the pigment of house walls that are predominantly white. It was 'the Surfacers'.

Atlantic rollers come pounding in to Tiree's many and long hard shell sand beaches, when the wind and weather co-operate. There is a large, shallow fresh water loch, Loch Bhasapol, inland by the secondary school, perfect for beginner wind-surfing lessons. It was a day of free lessons for all of the school children on the island. Translucent butterfly wings skimmed and scudded and flopped in a melee of rainbow triangles.

Gaelic speaking activity holidays, the Feis (Gaelic Festival), as well as wind surfing are all expanding activities on Tiree. It was the first island on the northwards peregrination where Gaelic was commonly talked in passing.

Not a lot of 'Soothmothers' here, as the Shetlanders would say. The wind is too strong.

Ballevullin

Scarinish

The Windy Gap.

Coll, *Colla, June 1*

approx population: 150
Land area: 28.75 sq. miles

There are all sorts of derogatory tales differentiating islanders. The Tiree man who walks permanently at an angle of 45 degrees on account of that wind; the Mull man who steps high on account of the bracken; and the Coll man who gets headaches when he visits Mull on account of the mountains. Coll and Tiree are very flat. But

Crossabol House
& the Graveyard falling
into the sea

there the similarity ends. The first impression of Tiree is of a South Seas atoll albeit cooler in temperature and minus date palms. Arriving from Oban the flat rockscape of the long uninhabited eastern coast of Coll looks most inhospitable. Half way along, the inlet of Loch Eatharna gives a glimpse of the tiny village of Arinagour. 'Good God! People actually *live* on this island?' say the round trippers.

Sometimes I am tempted not to tell about the miles long strands and little cowrie shell-scalloped beaches, sand dunes, machair and lily lochs that lie beyond the baleful moonscape. To keep them private. But it doesn't seem to matter; you will always find a beach on Coll that is completely deserted even during Glasgow Fair Fortnight. Each one has its very own special character and devotees.

Coll Parish Church Manse
The Housing Action ·····

Robert & Ruth's back
door step

As we talked, Peggy's cat ran off with a crab's leg. "That's nothing" said Ruth. "There was the day the seagull took a whole lobster. I chased it the length of the village street. Low flying it was on account of the weight. It dropped it in the end.

Kenneth's Rare Breeds
— quite undisturbed
as I ambled
thro'
the park

BREACHACHA

COLL

ARINAGOUR village street, the yachties and the sheep.

The other contrast with Tiree is in the social structure. There are few traditional working crofts, it having been an island of landlords and incoming Lowland tenant dairy farmers in the now forgotten era of the Coll Cheeses. Those days are gone and nowadays everyone on Coll seems to be their own landlord on some venture or other. And not a serf in sight.

The architecture reflects the diversity and dissimilarity with Tiree even further. Coll has everything from the whitewashed thatched crofthouse and residential caravans to the wooden shooting lodge, holiday house and castles—two in number.

Yet Tiree is the administrative headquarters for both islands and that is where the elected councillor responsible for both islands lives. Coll's population is only one sixth of Tiree's.

There has always been a kind of country cousin attitude by Tiree towards Coll. During the Second World War, Tiree was one of the bases for the Halifax Bombers of Coastal Command. Peacetime inherited the diesel powered electricity, a good pier, an extensive military airfield which provided the basis for the present daily air link to Glasgow. Eventually Coll was connected to Tiree's electricity supply via the sound of Gunna. A faltering dependency at times.

Now, the Collachs, if they so chanced to think on it, are in the advantage. Mains electricity, underwater from Mull, reaches Tiree by coming overland on Coll. Another set of skyline poles so quickly lurching at an angle away from their initial upright position in the bog and sand terrain. A hallmark of the Outer Isles. Somehow Coll and Tiree belong more to those islands than they do to the Glasgow-centred region of Strathclyde.

I had once lived on Coll for nearly ten years and known it since I was seventeen. For the purposes of this project I found it very difficult to be objective. The five days allocated were filled with visiting—*de rigeur*—and all thoughts of in-depths soliloquies on deserted beaches were denied.

Coll people are very hospitable. And it takes a long time for the kettle to boil.

IMPORTANT NOTICE TO VISITORS TO THE WESTERN ISLES

ROAD SIGNS IN THE WESTERN ISLES

As part of it's policy in preserving the Gaelic language, the Western Isles Council has adopted a policy of Gaelic place names throughout the Western Isles, except in the anglicized areas of Stornoway and Benbecula where the names are in both Gaelic and English

"The Ramp 'jammed'. CASTLEBAY Arrival 9.00P.M Perishables hand off-loaded. Vehicles and owners go on to S. Uist at 10.30pm. for Repair

Barra, *Barraigh, June 8*

approx population: 1,364
Land area: 20 sq. miles

With hindsight, the journey and stay on Barra fitted the whole 'Whisky Galore' image that the media loves to perpetuate.

It·was a very bad crossing, everyone coping in their own way. Heads down or glasses of spirits up and down. One poor woman sat in a daze of disbelief. She had mistakenly walked onto the Barra boat at Oban whilst her nephew had driven their car onto the intended Mull ferry. She couldn't understand why she was unable to find him in the cafeteria, as planned, when the boat got under way. And she couldn't get a cup of tea whilst waiting for him to turn up as he had her bag in the car . . .

The true horror of the situation slowly dawned as Mull, only a half hour

CASTLEBA[Y]
A Sunday Afterno[on]
& then the coal boat
came in . . . .

crossing, slipped past. 'It's happened before', said a laconic holiday home owner going to South Uist, the next island on from Barra. The immensity of the gaff was further compounded when the poor woman realized the full consequence.

The new *Claymore* serves Barra and South Uist stopping overnight in Lochboisdale in South Uist before sailing back next morning to Oban.

We fed her cups of tea and lent her books. The Purser provided her with a berth should she want to sleep the whole nightmare away long before natural bedtime.

As the boat heaved her way out over the Minch, it was announced that due to hoist problems no vehicles could land on Barra. It was hoped that repairs could be effected at Lochboisdale during the night. More heads went down and a lot more glasses went up and down. A young American woman blessed with elegant sea legs delighted in the whole drama. She was working for a U.S. travel advertising agency. 'I sell islands. It's a fun trip today, isn't it?' she quipped, ignoring a screaming family with three under-five children that had been travelling from Glasgow since 9.00 a.m.

The crossing to Barra normally takes six hours. For those of us with vehicles on that occasion it took fourteen hours. That woman who had missed half her weekend on Mull then had a further six or seven hours to go before joining up, no doubt apprehensively, with her long lost relative.

The van and I both arrived indisposed in Barra. Me with lack of sleep and possibly too much up and down arm movements; the van with a drained battery refusing to hold a charge.

The regulator had to be replaced. It had to be ordered by post from the mainland. It was best not to drive the van. Daily, to begin with, I cycled to the mechanic's house to check on delivery. He always seemed to be in the bath. After ten days of 'maybe tomorrow' from his wife, I gave up and fell into the glazed condition of all true islanders dependent on the heartless mysteries of mainland supplying.

'Mañana', particularly associated with the Western Isles, is simply a method of self restraint that cools boiling fury and stabilizes the flow of apoplectic blood to the brain. The further away from main centre supplies the more evident the manifestation.

There was nothing for it but to get on my bike.

Barra was en fête; the Feis (Gaelic Festival) was in full swing. Bagpipes practised out the back of crofts; and night long ceilidhs, essential for post performance assessment, were required research for the three TV crews that got paler in the jowls as the days went by, despite the return of the heatwave. A busload of elderly Americans on a castles tour of Scotland—I'm sure it was the weight of their bus that jammed the hoist—roved in varying stages of wealthy decrepitude, Pentax extensions permanently attached to the end of their noses.

On Sunday, Castlebay was the hub of all activity.

I sat under a parasol outside the Cafe. The bay was alive with sailing dinghies and surfers. The Barra Lifeboat and an Air Sea Rescue helicopter were practising winch drops. Laboriously wending their way through all this were the participants of the annual Bathtub Race.

At the pier the coal boat had to get out of the way to allow the first of the Sunday day return ferry sailings to the Outer Isles to get alongside. The *Pioneer* had set off from Mallaig packed with more mainland relatives than tourists. The pier was mobbed.

The Gaelic conversation all around, with the parasol, added to the Mediterranean feel of the day. It seemed a very joyous thing to be a Catholic.

All that was lacking was the MacNeil of MacNeil's trumpeter up on the castle rampart.

That evening Fathers Callum and Fraser hosted a ceilidh at Northbay Hall. In between performances of clarsach, song and dance, children fluttered and festooned themselves around the two priests like the very birds of St Francis of Assisi. Eighty-five year old Peigi after much gentle cajoling from Father Callum was persuaded to sing. After a few false starts in a wavery thin voice of great purity she got under way, and the whole hall was silent in fervent loving support. Soon she was fired by the communal chorus repeats. 'There'll be no stopping her now' smiled Father Callum with a wry, crinkly-eyed smile. Religion on Barra is paternalistically reassuring and kind.

Northbay is close to a new and wavering fish meal factory. Smells and arguments galore. In certain changes of wind, the washing has to be hastily taken in. Often it has to be rewashed.

Holiday house owners are notorious for dining off quaint native tales, the winter long; not those with properties in the environs of the fish meal factory. You

cannot cull any clever jokes from out of that smell.

'But it is giving employment!' How often I heard that phrase in defence of commercial implants, structural—and human.

I had just finished reading Catriona McNeil's newly published memoirs of a Barra childhood. She was born in 1911 and I was swept along with her nostalgia for the days gone by of the thriving herring industry based in Castlebay. There must have been a ferocious smell then, too. I wonder who complained?

The rate at which we disregard the future of the fruits of the sea, we will soon have no need for fish meal or processing factories. But how long do Governments go on handing out subsidies to non viable communities? Is it, as ever, a matter of compromised choice?

Burdened with such heavy thoughts I decided it was time to go over to Vatersay. Mañana still obtained concerning the innards of the van.

Vatersay, *Bhatarsaigh*

approx population: 72
Land area: 3 sq. miles

If the Tiree folk look upon Collachs as country cousins, then the Barra folk look upon Vatersachs as country cousins once, twice or thrice times removed. The shop—a Co-Chommun (Community Co-operative), P.O., church, school and village hall are scattered in isolation over a sparsely populated island necessitating long walks for whatever service is required. There are few vehicles on Vatersay. The Co-Chommun minibus clocks up surprisingly high mileages on the five miles of road.

The great focus of attention on the island was 'The Wedding' soon to take place. Patricia, related onto the island but brought up on the mainland had returned to work in the Co-Chommun shop. Romance had followed. She was soon to be married to Donald, a local fisherman; one of the many bachelors on Vatersay. The wedding was seen as a very symbolic event in a community precariously near voluntary mass emigration to the bright lights of neighbouring Castlebay. There are high expectations of the union of the couple.

Passing the school overlooking the brilliant white sands of Vatersay Bay it was playtime and the handful of children hung over the fence obviously delighted to see a visitor. 'Where do you come from?' they chanted, in heavily accented English. Gaelic is alive and well on Vatersay. The teacher will shout out to them in the playground if she hears them speaking English. Changed days from the childhood of their grandparents who were belted for uttering a word of Gaelic, their one and only language.

From Vatersay you can look south to the scatter of The Bishop's Isles now uninhabited save for sheep. Mingulay, that most mellifluous of island names, being the last to be evacuated before the Great War.

The coming of the causeway to Vatersay will stop history repeating itself, aid transport of supplies—and bulls, and facilitate Vatersay's first ever council rubbish collection. The cars and that American tourist bus will come too.

I never made the wedding but had a taste of the Vatersay hospitality that lasted till dawn. A fishing boat took 'Barrachs' back over the bay as the cream light from the East filtered into the inky blue. Stars still shone at the edge of the sky.

The flat afterdeck of a prawn creel boat is an excellent platform for two pipers and an eightsome reel.

We danced our way into the new day.

Eriskay, *Eirisgeigh, June 20*

approx population: 200
Land area: 4.50 sq. miles

Still being vanless, in a motorised capacity, it made sense to go to Eriskay on the foot passenger ferry from Eoligarry at the north end of Barra.

VATERSAY   The New Church Door
& Wall

There, white sands stretched under the sea in gradations of blues and greens, from jade to deepest indigo blue. An emerald-keeled dinghy piled high with turquoise netted creels and a navy blue fisherman completed the bi-tonal picture.

On sunny days blue surrounds Eriskay. Marine blue. Madonna blue. Our Lady and the sea axiomatically entwined. The very altar table in St Michael's Church is supported on the bow of a boat.

The analogy with a Greek island is very strong in Eriskay. The land rises steeply and rockily from the sand-girt beaches dipping quickly into those evocative blues. St Michael's, like a monastery, is the highest building on the island. The houses, however, do not cluster precariously round for protection. Marauding pirates are less recent in the history of the Hebrides.

There is still a lot of fishing on Eriskay. Another Co-Chommun runs the village shop and diesel supply base for fishing boats from all over the Hebrides. In the shop, priceless (in effect £80–£90) handknitted traditional seamen's jumpers, each stitch a symbolic legend in itself, hang beside the baked beans and Cup-a-soups. Will the younger women of the island keep on producing these especial single coloured garments? Mary Flora in the Post Office was mending a twelve year old jumper belonging to 'a famous actor', returned for loving care and uplift. They *are* priceless.

For a little island Eriskay certainly has made its name, what with Bonnie Prince Charlie's first landing on Scottish soil at Coilleag a Phrionnsa, its love song, jumpers, ponies and Whisky Galore wreck.

In the pony world there is much contention as to what exactly defines an Eriskay pony. Blood or birth place? The indigenous stock on the island is much diluted and some claim that the purest ponies are to be found in southeast England.

On a hillside, old Linda, tethered at this time of year for carrying the peats, looked all that an Eriskay pony should be to me. Low slung and all. Her fiery nine month old son, Beauty, dark brown in sharp spicy contrast to his mother's milk-grey coat would lose his camouflage colouring and crimpy gold-dusted mane as he matured. In years to come his whinnying might be heard of a dark night going over to a horsebox in South Uist?

The Politician was the name of the Second World War cargo boat which wrecked its way into fame and other people's fortune. Inspired by the event which happened in the narrows between Eriskay and South Uist, Compton McKenzie wrote *Whisky Galore*. He lived on Barra and that island has taken the full kudos—or brunt, depending on sensibilities—of association with the sinking of the whisky-laden ship. (Galore, incidentally, is a corruption of the Gaelic word gu lèor, meaning plenty.)

Eriskay's first ever pub of dreaded kithouse originality trades on the event and is called 'Am Politician'. The modern decor is incongruously enlivened by several filthy old bottles containing what looks like ancient pee retrieved from the wreck on the sea bed. The liquid actually smells citrusy. The taste? Better left to the imagination . . .

After a while, in the nature of all hostelries with the right amount of *uisge-beatha gu lèor,* it doesn't matter what the surroundings are like.

North Smerclate
S. Uist.

South Uist, *Uibhist a Deas, June 23*

approx population: 2,430
Land area: 141 sq. miles

The longer I travelled in the islands the more I felt the need of recourse to that *uisge beatha gu leor* (golden liquid). The regulator had arrived and been fitted on the van by the time I got back to Barra. At last mobility—and the unlimited use of the internal light, the radio and tape cassette. And then the sliding door fell off.

The mechanic in the bath was going on his holidays.

Tied on with elasticated spider ropes, the door, the van and I arrived at Lochboisdale in South Uist in need of strong support.

West of Lochboisdale, there is a suntrap hollow in the sand dunes at the end of the longest beach in the Hebrides; twenty miles of sand and surf leading to infinity. There, sanity was cradled below the canopy awning that is elemental to the Uists—the sky.

South Uist was also sea and birds. And purple-hazed mountains to the north. Machair, the height and density to give a gnome a forest; myriads of glittering inland lochs where hundreds of swans and waterlilies vied in whiteness. In high summer, anywhere in the Hebrides, there is such a feeling of abundance and largesse after the long dark, depression-swept winter.

PEAT BANKS
Ludaig/South
Glendale
S. UIST. June 26.

Entrance Porch   *June 28*   WEST HIGHLAND CROFTERS & FARMERS LTD.

Fledgling peewits, maybe drugged with the heady, almost sickly sweet, perfume of the swards of wildflowers, repeatedly pittered, innocently suicidal, on to the metalled road. The adult birds ran parallel in the long grass, high pitched in distress. Once a cat skulked in the ditch. Flat-eared, it ignored the screaming divebombs of the adult birds, eyes never wavering off the little ball of speckled fluff on matchstick stilts.

I never could find a name for that great long shellsand beach. I camped at several points along its length. To be at Rudha Ardvule, the most westerly point in South Uist, and watch a giant fireball of a midsummer sun slowly slip off the edge of the world is almost too much for the human condition to bear.

Fulmars were nesting in low sand dunes below Askernish House. An unusual site as these birds belong to the cliffs. Their numbers have greatly increased since the evacuation of St Kilda—seventy miles due west. Hence colonisation of other islands, cliffless or not. The sand dunes on South Uist must have seemed like a soft option to the fulmars.

It would be very easy to miss the experience of the vastness of that western seaboard if one kept to the main road. Straight as the swans fly, it goes the length of South Uist, then links to Benbecula, Grimsay and North Uist by causeways.

Not all that long ago travellers had to wait at the edge of each island for the tide to go out before crossing the hard lugworm-cast sands. The safest route over the fords indicated by markers can still be seen. Less than an hour's drive will now take you from Lochboisdale in South Uist to Lochmaddy in North Uist without so much as getting your feet wet. The transmigration will not only be physical. Your soul will have safari-ed through Sunday festivals and football matches, wayside altars of pastel-faded kitsch, smiley priests and a lot of Virgin Marys on mantelpieces, shop counters and mountainsides. Ending finally in Lochmaddy, strait-laced, Sabbatarian and extremely serious.

It is quite important, for your soul's sake, to start at the end that you would prefer not to be the terminus.

Benbecula from Carinish
Benbecula best viewed from a distance.....

Benbecula, *Beinn a'Bhaoghla, June 29*

approx population: 2,242
Land area: 30 sq. miles

Benbecula is pivotal not only to the religions of the Uists but to their administration, education and economy. It has little else to recommend it save the new Magnificat of Linicleit community school. Hew Lorimer's colossus of a Virgin Mary and Child, towering over the south side of the island, is lower than the skyline symbol of the predominant force on Benbecula. Her Majesty's Forces, in the uniform of the Royal Artillery. Address: The Rocket Range.

Ignoring the questionable validity of shooting millions of pounds worth of practice missiles into the Atlantic, monitored by the radar station on St Kilda, the Army are seen as a friendly and very beneficial force of occupation. The NAAFI supermarket is the only one in Britain open to the general public. Gaelic gossiped in and out the gondolas; Brum and Cockney accents added up at the checkout. The well-stocked shelves of staple and sophisticated goods were a culinary Aladdin's cave after weeks of limited fare. Tagliatelli Verdi and Lapsang Souchong tea!

Posters on the way out offered details of forthcoming events: Pony Club, Keep Fit, Swimming, Diving, Running. That night there was to be a fashion show in aid of funds for Great Ormond Street Hospital for Children in London.

'The Army wives run everything on Benbecula', said my companion as we sat in the gym hall of the Army Base, converted for the evening into a dimly lit night club. Candles were on tables; flowers draped the catwalk. Everyone from the Brigadier to the squaddies in best casual civvies. The locals spruce in anticipation. Behind, the length of the far wall, the Army Catering Corps had prepared a sumptuous buffet.

The Padre, in evening suit with crimson cummerbund, was Master of Ceremonies.

The models were Army and local, and had been professionally rehearsed. Those army wives again. Two young local lads were top class adverts for Next, quite at ease with the catwalk and audience. One, I'm sure, last seen in a baker's hat at McLean's Bakery. The other—proved correct—behind the counter in the bank. He was a very good piper too.

Sitting in the shadows, hiding my walking boots well under my chair, the double incongruity struck home. Here I was in Ultima Thule and there was no heather growing out of anyone's ears save my own.

Nearby, loud confident English accents emphasised the colonial outpost feel of the Army in Benbecula. Far from home the island must seem like a distant outpost of Empire. But the natives are friendly and can all speak English.

And I was going to stay friendly with the Army. I hoped they would help me get out to St Kilda in the next supply ship in September.

Grimsay, *Griomasaigh*

approx population: 212
Land area: 2.50 sq. miles

Little Grimsay just north of Benbecula was a regular base camp retreat for the weeks I was in the Uists. In actuality the van was sited on the even tinier island adjacent—Gearradubh. Causeways link up the fretwork of the little islands of the Uists as well as the big.

On Gearradubh, Lachie's house is even on its own island, the size of the house and garden. A latter day crannog . . . The tractor parked by the causeway track can be awash at the high spring tides.

In Lachie's childhood there was no causeway to the house or to neighbouring Grimsay. He and his brothers and sisters were ferried over to school in Grimsay in a 'cobble'—a flat bottomed boat. 'It was only a few hundred yards. Though wild it could be in winter'.

That day it had been announced that the Gearradubh and Grimsay children would no longer attend the school in Grimsay. It was to be closed. They were to go to Carinish in North Uist, only four miles distant. Protests were more against loss of identity than local facility.

GAELIC
PROVERB:

"He'll not sell
his hen on
a rainy
day"

GRIMSAY

Sandbank
(Lachie's) GEARRADUBH   The Causeway built '75   Shenoval · GRIMSA

Grimsay is the size of island a serious jogger could jog round before breakfast. The Major does. One of the increasing number of Army personnel who have bought property whilst stationed at Benbecula, he would like a permanent posting and certainly has full intentions of returning on retirement from 'tours of duty'.

Being more or less resident beside Lachie's peat bank, I collected a lodger. A tiny black and white moggy, miniature for her adult age. She would arrive like clockwork every morning and was not interested in food. But what paroxysms of drooling ecstasy she would go into on being stroked. Unfortunately, she had a nasty cold. She was very good at catching the flies that seemed to be breeding in the van, however.

Her daily visits and Lachie's two visitor-friendly collies brought on pangs of homesickness compounded, not relieved, by giving Lachie a hand one day bringing in the winter peats on the back of the tractor.

Lachie called Gearradubh 'Baile ma tha ma thogair.' The Township of So What Does it Matter.

It was time to move on.

Berneray, *Beàrnaraigh Na Hearadh, July 6*

approx population: 136
Land area: 446 acres
Berneray is an exemplary little island.

The owner seldom visits; he asks for minimal rent and is totally respectful of the crofting islanders' wishes concerning development. 'If anyone wanted to build a hotel or fancy guest house on Berneray he would reply politely and say if it is what the people of Berneray want then I will discuss it,' proudly recounted one local. The islander was also adamant that there were no 'foreign' holiday houses on the island. 'The holiday houses belong to *relatives*'. A different matter altogether.

Berneray lacks nothing for the perfect island idyll—save peat. What it wants in fossil fuel it makes up for in fodder. On the machair, cleared of sheep and cattle for the summer, I waded through buttercups, yellow vetch, ladies' bedstraw, clover, daisy, ragwort and plantain to name but an amateur few. The fertile machair land is where the vegetables are grown in the Outer Isles. Here, also, on Berneray, is a royal potato patch to be found.

For Berneray is another Prince Charlie island. Not for the beginnings of a regal ego trip, as in Eriskay all those years ago, but for a private time, free of fads and followers.

The people of Berneray kept the whole episode of Prince Charles' 'crofting holiday' a total secret. After the royal bird had flown, the media descended. £10,000 was offered to any islander willing to go to London to be in a feature already entitled 'The Prince and the Pauper'. £10 offered for just one of the potatoes fruited from the Prince's spring labours. Nobody went and nobody sold a potato.

I am quite sure that His Royal Highness will have already arranged for his tatties to be uplifted. *Britannia*, no doubt, will convoy them on their long way south.

'Daddy's Hebridean chips for tea!' the little princes will cheer.

Fair Game .
As I sketched, he filmed. Me.
Berneray

North Uist, *Uibhist a Tuath*

approx population: 1,520
Land area: 118 sq. miles

Islands have physical boundaries that make it far easier to retain old ways and habits far longer than is possible in more accessible regions.

When the causeways were being proposed to link South and North Uist to Benbecula, North Uist was very apprehensive of free access to the South. Or reluctant, rather, for the converse flow of free movement. Travelling on a Sunday in North Uist is still frowned upon by some.

The natural partners of North Uist are Harris and Lewis, the last bastions of radical Protestantism. But the Sound of Harris is too wide to bridge. So North Uist bravely and seriously upholds the faith. The change is palpable when one arrives on North Uist from the south. Markedly so on a Sunday.

It must be said that not all the people living in these islands are caught up in spiritual entrenchment. Not nearly enough, the faithful would say. The media loves to exaggerate the polarity. Hence Barra's hedonistic excesses are contrasted with Lewis's black-garbed piousness.

Of the 75,520 acres that make up North Uist, 8,000 are fresh water lochs. Lochmaddy is the capital and terminal for the ferries to Harris and Skye. If one religiously (!) walks in and out the indentations of its shore-line you will have covered forty three miles and still be in hailing distance of the Tourist Office.

South of Lochmaddy, a fraction of these lochs and lochans are scattered, like silvery jigsaw pieces, in and around miles of orderly peat banks. Like Lachie in Grimsay, everyone was intent in getting the peats in before the next break in the weather. Thunderclouds and flies had been hovering irritably.

Images of peat gathering are often associated with creels and bent-backed peasant women; men with jutting pipes and braces. And poverty. Only the upper classes used to import coal to the islands. Then came the electricity and the oil. And the rising prices.

Smart cars as well as tractors and vans were parked nose-to-tail in the lay-bys

N. Uist
Agricultural Society
Sheepdog Trials

GRIMSAY / N. UIST
Causeway.
Van rocking & bog cotton flying in high winds.

at the peatbanks. Owners, some rubber-gloved, filled brightly coloured plastic bags with next winter's cheaper, if hard won, fuel. Bag after bag still to be hauled to the roadside. Like colourful brochs some stacks will stay there all winter—single bags collected when needed. Others are carted home en masse to build great black insulating extensions to gable ends.

The west of North Uist is like the west of all of the 'Long Isle', as this skein of islands used to be called. Beaches, dunes and machair. The thunder grumbled away leaving a deceptive calm. It was a day of unique clarity, later reported in the papers. Quite by chance, I saw, incomprehensibly at first, the jewel flash of precious stones on the line of the west horizon. Glittering turquoises, emeralds. St Kilda. Like a flirtatious reminder.

The day of freak clear vision gave way to cold northerly winds and lateral salt-soaked rains. It cleared enough to shine on the North Uist Sheepdog Trials on Holsta machair but froze the judges' note-taking fingers. Many forays were made into the refreshments tent for shelter and sustenance. But not a drop of the hard stuff in sight. Sheepdog Trials are serious affairs. 'No bitches on heat allowed in field,' either.

The Small Isles, *Na h-Eileanan Beaga, July 18*

approx population: 130
Land area: 57.50 sq. miles

For all sorts of complicated reasons I decided not to travel on to Harris and Lewis from North Uist. There was still Skye and the Small Isles to do and I had this notion to end the trip in Lewis, the most northerly of all the islands. And it had been arranged that I would get that Army boat from South Uist to St Kilda in early September.

I had a month and a half to finish the Inner Hebrides. The new once-fortnightly Sunday sailing from Mallaig to Barra was the perfect connection for the Small Isles.

Driving south through North Uist it almost felt sinful heading for the wrong kind of a Sunday service.

From the top of the Sgurr of Eigg, a conning tower of pitchstone lava, the intimacy of the neighbouring islands and mainland is apparent.

Miniscule Muck lies flat to the south like the proverbial pancake; the dramatic mountain silhouette of Rum blanks out Canna, low-lying to the North West. All four islands, so disparate in ownership and landscape, are linked together by the hundred and thirty passenger Cal Mac mailboat *Lochmor*, based at Mallaig, Another independently owned boat, the *Shearwater*, also serves Eigg and Muck from Arisaig.

I sat for hours watching the tiny water beetle washes of the two boats glinting on the sea's surface far below. Captain Swanson on the bridge of the *Lochmor* would be in the full eloquent flood of his tannoy-ed guided tour.

Going to the Small Isles is like stepping back in time. And the 'stepping' has got to be co-ordinated. Only at Canna is there a pier to accommodate the *Lochmor*; at the other three islands, weather permitting, a ferry boat comes alongside—and you jump.

Lack of car ferries, pubs or mains electricity have helped the Small Isles to retain their timeless quality. Yet Eigg is nearer to the mainland than Coll and Tiree. An underwater electricity cable then linked to the others of the group would be no insurmountable task.

There seems to be a quiet conspiracy of *laissez-faire*. Agriculturally in Eigg, where the bracken is a hundred times worse than it was when Fraser Darling made warning noises in his West Highland Survey in 1955. In Nature Conservancy owned Rum there are positive steps taken to control access to and on the island. Canna has just been gifted to the National Trust. Little Muck, which is no more than an island farm, is the only one of the four where there is no outside check—barring the sea.

Seventy year old Dr MacLean, based on Eigg, has served the Small Isles for thirty years. He refuses to retire until he is assured that he will be replaced. He can get no confirmation.

All in all there is an aura of great uncertainty as to the future of these islands. I hope the dark silent dominance of Rum is not an indicator. Their beauty together and individually should not become exclusive.

Muck, *Eilean nam Muc*

approx population: 19
Land area: 2.50 sq. miles
If you have to be storm bound, where better than on Muck?

Stormbound Day 2

Ewen telling us that the forecast for tomorrow is not good but he is sure that the boat will come.

We are all, save Monica, replete with lobster.

Muck's Square of cows

Ewen McEwen's guesthouse, furnishings, menus and hospitality are all homemade—in the most sophisticated sense of the word. A house-party atmosphere obtained: maybe encouraged by the tiny size of the island and latterly by our adventurous condition.

Ewen bakes bread and rolls in time for breakfast. And will go out to his creels for a lobster for dinner should you wish. In between he weeds the vegetables and dusts out the bedrooms, and wonders when the storm will let the old guests leave, and have the new ones stranded at Mallaig or Arisaig given up waiting . . . ?

Muck can be walked round in a day. Its deceptively high Ben looks down on a patchwork of silage-cut fields, Walt Disney yellow and green. The force nine gale had blasted off the clouds and rain. Brilliant sun and a fierce wind kept the white horses out at sea whipped into a frenzy. Already there was the purple haze of flowering bell heather.

The castle on Rum is *the* historical building that must be visited. On Muck it has to be the telephone box. It still functions through a human operator in Mallaig. Polite instructions belonging to the days of courtesy, advise on the use of buttons A and B and not being too selfish as to the duration of the call.

No Boat Today

MUCK
Telephone
Box.

The Storm Came
Tues. Day of
supposed departure

The Top House.
Cleadale Eigg

Eigg, *Eige*

approx population: 70
Land area: 8.50 sq. miles

There are two sides to Eigg; the Estate and the Big House at Galmisdale, and the crofting township over the mid-shoulder of the island at Cleadale. In July both halves almost disappear under the virulent and sickly sweet-smelling bracken, an uncontrolled inheritance from the cessation of mono-culture beef farming in days gone by. Now, only sheep wander by, decorated with ruffs of bracken foliage. They say the grass is sweeter underneath. Above the crofts on the rampart cliffs of Beinn Bhuidhe, a natural column, God's finger, points upward. In admonition?

The craftshop at the pier could do a fast line in Eigg-timers, but the sand on Eigg is better employed. The Singing Sands, a fine white beach on beyond Cleadale, has what must be the most beautiful view in the Hebrides—the fabulous landmass and peaks of neighbouring Rum. But it is famous for its sands which make a sort of tuneful squeak when walked upon, particularly at the end of a hot day.

In between the two halves is the social centre of the community—the shop and Post Office. 'You'll not be in a hurry'? asked Angus, as we wheezed up the hill in his rust red landrover after collecting me from the boat. 'We'll just wait for the mail to be sorted'. Maybe Eigg-timers should have no sand in them ...

Inside and outside the long building are a row of seats, full on boat days with locals and visitors, there as much for 'the crack' as for supplies. The shop has a licence to sell beer so the seats also constitute an alfresco bar on fine days. Unfortunately the emptied containers of liquid refreshment do not disappear as quickly as the glow they induce.

It is unfair to pick on any one island concerning this subject. Nowhere is it worse than on Barra where row upon row of disused cars lie on the sand dunes. But Eigg is such a beautiful island it makes the blight even more disfiguring although one Morris Minor roadside wreck was almost picturesque with its garlands of brambles. And maybe the bracken is a blessing in disguise. For the summer months at least.

The Black Box - the phone box
Eigg

A'Chruagach
Prettiest Wreck I've ever
seen....

and the brambles will be good this September

Eigg sheep
Ruffed in
bracken

July 22
Kildonnan Eigg.

Already the purple bloom of flowering
bell heather

One of the many
KINLOCH CASTLE bathrooms
(Shanks of Barrhead)

Fireplace

Rum, *Rum*

approx population: 30
Land area: 42 sq. miles

All thirty people living on Rum are employed by the Nature Conservancy. The ferry boat ticket is called a landing card and one is in no doubt as to the restrictions imposed on all visitors. Thus, beyond the village and castle all is wilderness. Walkers can go over to Harris, the place where Sir George Bullough's extraordinary Parthenon-like mausoleum sits on the edge of wild cliffs, but not to beautiful Kilmory Bay except for Sunday afternoons—it takes two and a half hours just to walk there. This is where the research station is for the 1,700 deer that inhabit Rum.

In late July, the early morning greeting of the islanders is always thus: 'They're going to be bad today'. Do they mean the day trippers from Mallaig? Marauding deer? Radio and television reception? No, it is the midges.

Midges on Rum have the bite of an eagle. Hooded, gloved and scarf-masked students of the natural sciences end up behaving most unnaturally. Even reduced unto tears. Earth shattering treatises are flung to the four winds or even set fire to for temporary respite.

Maybe it is for our own sanity that the NCC restricts access.

My escape from the midges was to the Castle. In stockinged feet, I was allowed to tiptoe around sketching whilst the guests were dining. This happily preserved Edwardian extravaganza is open to the public and depending on the pocket, there is a choice of accommodation from Lady Monica's boudoir bedroom to the maid's attic bedroom. But remember, Sir George Bullough had central heating put into the kennels but not into the servants' quarters.

Possibly, there is still swimming about in the Sound of Rum, the last living link with the pre 1914–18 glory that was Kinloch Castle. Four years ago a turtle was hauled up in a fisherman's net off the West Coast of Skye. The Castle's turtle pond was drained at the end of the Great War and the inmates set free in Kinloch Bay. The waters of the West Coast are too cold for them to breed but at least one hardy and aged survivor may still be paddling along. And I hope not too lonely.

Departing Rum
July 30

ENTRANCE TO
CANNA
HOUSE

Iain McKinnon

The Old Catholic Church. Canna

THE BLUE SPIDER
The long centre communion table & spider's web & blue spider
presbyterian Church Canna.

Canna, *Canaigh*

approx population: 22
Land area: 4.50 sq. miles

Arriving at Canna one could be understandably mistaken as to the proclivities of
the inhabitants. Cliffs by the pier are gaily daubed with names and numbers. Is this
an Alcatraz detention centre for underpass graffiti louts? Certainly there is an
obsession with girls' names. It turns out to be the signatures of generations of
yachties and fishermen each one vying for a higher or more inaccessible site.

'In the old days the paint faded after a while' rued Margaret Fay Shaw,
American folklorist wife of the Gaelic scholar John Lorne Campbell. They have
recently gifted the island to the National Trust and the first 'private' signs have gone
up on the Campbells' gates. Bilingually, of course.

The first National Trust cruise ship would soon be arriving, disgorging hundreds
of visitors in one fell swoop. Winnie's Post Office was well stocked with T-shirts
and sweatshirts as well as stamps and postcards.

Sanday is attached to Canna by a wooden bridge and guarded by a stained glass
madonna set in sparkling white stone. On Sanday are two families and the two
pupil school, and the sadly deteriorating mini cathedral. And there is the perfect
example of an anomaly that is, ironically, particular to the Small Isles—and to St
Kilda: a noisy generator pounded outside a house that had a Greenpeace sticker on
the front window. With so many more electric gadgets in everyday use these aural
pollutants are on from dawn to dusk in some places.

The thumping of the generators may have another side effect. I have never
seen so many rabbits as there were on Sanday and Canna.

View from
Canna House
— another kind
of an eye on
the Hebrides?

Ang. 2

Skye, *An t-Eilean Sgitheanach, August 3*

approx population: 8,500
Land area: 535 sq. miles

How could I possibly cover an island the size and diversity of Skye in the limited time that I had?

I was beginning to tire. At intervals, friends on Skye provided beds and baths and meals with tables set with cutlery, serviettes and wine glasses. There is a limit to fry-ups in the back of a van with a newspaper over one's knee. I had softened, living vanless, on the Small Isles.

The best crossing to Skye is from Mallaig to Armadale. It really is going 'over the sea to Skye' compared to the five minute Kyleakin crossing. The Sleat peninsula is lush and beautiful with a stunning aspect of the Cuillins from the little known hamlets of Toskavaig and Totavaig. A steep winding road scares off most of the tourists, of which there are thousands in August—as there are midges. These two subjects were major topics of conversation.

TARSAVAIG GOOSE SHED
Aug 6

Already, like the blooming heather on Muck, there were signs of the turn of the summer; muscular podded iris, orange rowan berries, green elderberries. Summer! It never fails to amaze me that tourists come to the Western Highlands and Islands of Scotland in the 'summer' month of August. Of course there were the odd sunny days but the overall memory is of midges weaving in and out of the waterfall warp of torrential rains. The van stank of candles and coils promising instant relief. The Skye midges are smaller than the Rum ones, but their beaks are sharper.

After researching THE PURPOSE OF MIDGES ON THIS PLANET at the well-stocked Clan Donald Field Centre Library (they are the basic food of the reed warbler) I went on to Sabhal Mòr Ostaig the Gaelic College. Why, I asked, are there so few references in literature and music to that tiny fly? It must have caused battles to be lost and love scenes to become farcical. Even Sorley McLean has not addressed himself to the issue. It must be because of the stoicism of the Gael; his mind on higher things though his body be tormented with misery.

I hoped the tourists would survive to come back in the spring or autumn, or even winter, to see the best of Skye.

Eddie, 'a refugee from the mainland', in his wind generated caravan, wondered 'if some of them *can* see'. Recently, an English couple, noticing yellowhammers at his bird table commented 'You feed wild canaries?' They went on to ask 'What river is that?' looking across the wide Sound of Sleat to the mainland.

But Murdo the ferryman at the Kylerhea crossing, laconic by nature, had the reverse to say. 'More ordinary folk as tourists nowadays—which is better. You learn more from them'. He fed a tame seagull. The tourists can recognise that without difficulty.

KYLERHEA
MURDO McKENZIE
at the Starboard
Helm of the
"GLENA HULISH"
built '69

30 years of ferrying

Isle Ornsay Aug 8
Hot gusting winds + another storm a-brewing

Oifis A'Phuist

Cuillins - after the 24 HR downpour -
from Tokavaig

7·30pm. Aug 5

7·30pm. Aug 5

TWO HRS LATER: 9·30pm. Aug 5
Cuillins from Totavaig

9·30pm. Aug 5

11·30 pm Aug 5

11·30 pm Aug 5

Next day — cloud right down to
sea level. Nothing to see
save a b/w black teated
cow
mowing away
the dew

KILMUIR SHOW
The President, Sir Iain McDonald
photographing the
Champion Tup.

Up from the narrows of Kylerhea is the Forestry Commission's Otter Haven, where visitors, if they are lucky, can watch otters. If not, the solar panelled information unit will play a tape of otters whistling and snuffling in their burrow. The instructions add a postscript. 'If the tape is not working properly, there has been a lack of sun'. Surprisingly, the otters communicated loud and clear the day I was there.

Parked by the old Broadford pier that night, bus parties were living it up in two of the neighbouring hotels. The Hokey-Cokey competed with live bagpipe music. A grey heron scraiked in disgust on the shore.

After Dunvegan and the encouraging news that the regular two hundred odd seals, after a slow spring start, had come back into the bay for the season, I made for the Piping College at Borreraig. I never realised how many ethnic pipes there are throughout the world. The development and survival of the Scottish pipes had a lot to do with the military uses of the instrument at the time of clan warfare. Subsequent Highland regiments carried on the tradition. In other countries pipes were generally played for secular or ceremonial occasions only.

The helicopter that had been hovering for days high up in the Quiraing—the wild, inhospitable mountains above Staffin—was shrugged off by the locals as 'some BBC thing or other.' Sgiathanachs are well-used to the cameras of TV crews.

By chance I had pulled up at a telephone box to try and work out what it was that dangled from the helicopter. Bundles of fencing stobs? A body?

A skid of brakes and a very flash car stopped by the box. It was the photographer and PR guy for an advertising agency. That suspended shape was the latest Peugeot estate car being airlifted off 'The Table', a flat plateau not much bigger than the vehicle itself. 'The Table' nestled behind 'The Needle', part of a row of monstrous jagged rock impalements, all of 1500 ft high.

They and the rest of the crew had been cramped up there for longer than expected, waiting for a dry day to film and photograph. Their brand new climbing boots were soaking wet. One of them had the unenviable task of having to phone up the advertising agency's accountant to ask for more expenses.

I would see the result of it all in the Sunday supplements in October, I was told.

English and foreign accents do not disappear once the tourists and silly season pass. After the tourists and the midges the next topic of conversation on Skye was 'the incomers'. Like a lot of the islands there are tensions between local and incomer. Figuratively, a melting pot 'is a state of dissolution preparatory to shaping anew'. Literally, it would be a waste to let it boil over.

At the Green House, a tasty restaurant run by a young English couple, the 'ceilidh' part of the evening, as it should, encouraged audience participation. It did not matter if it was clog dancing, Gaelic mouth music or Nigerian folk song. It was all for sharing.

There are a lot of people like that in Skye. Working hard, especially on plots of land that have such a limited growing season. In Glendale, where the croft land is freehold and belongs to the community, English and foreign accents are well to the fore. Some leave in time, battered down by the weather and their own intransigence in refusing to understand or respect the indiginous culture.

It should all be a two way process without presumptions on either side.

Raasay, *Ratharsair*

approx population: 180
Land area: 30 sq. miles

Raasay lies in the lee of Skye, gratefully cut off from the diverse complicated issues of its big neighbour, Skye. A once a week shopping trip to the supermarkets in Portree is quite enough for some.

Religion can hold a community together. So long as all are agreed on which one. Raasay is strictly Sabbitarian. The notice at the playing fields reminds those that might forget. PLEASE DO NOT USE THIS PLAYING FIELD ON SUNDAYS. Further along past Raasay House—now an Adventure Centre—there is another notice that conjures up wicked thoughts, TEMPTATION HILL WALK. It dates long back to the days of *priests*, of course.

Raasay is a perfect rambling island. There is also all that the Adventure Centre can offer. From strenuous to gentle the island provides a variety of walks, always with the hills of Skye dominating the western horizon. In the woods near the village I picked a couple of dinners of chanterelle mushrooms.

The road twists up and down more crazily the further north it goes. No wonder the Council gave up before they got to Callum's house leaving him the heroic task of completing the job single-handed. Callum is dead now, his widow moved to the village at Inverarish. The house shut up; the geraniums a peaceful pink in the porch. 'He used my barrow' said an elderly neighbour, now the last one living permanently in the remote wild spot.

The van rocked in the night, up at that isolated north end. More gales. Summer was definitely gone. By 9.30 p.m. it was pitch dark except for the lights of

Applecross on the mainland to the east. Back out with the sleeping bag *and* the duvet. And the thick socks.

Next day there was a silence about Raasay that was not only to do with the dying of summer and the fact that it was half-day closing in the shop. There had been 'an interment' after a funeral in Portree. Two Skye or mainland men with black ties and suits walked hesitantly up the village street looking for old acquaintances' houses.

End of the metalled rd.
N. Fearns ?
Raasay

Aug 24

SCADABAY

Mrs Martin's
doorway
with dyed sheep's
wool & a ginger cat.

Harris, *Na Hearadh, August 26*

approx population: 2,451
Land area: 90 sq. miles

Sailing over to Harris from Uig in Skye the weather was flat calm after all the rain
and gales. The bleakness of the terrain was shocking after the trees and lawns—and
chanterelles—of Raasay. I had forgotten the harsh eastern face of the Outer Isles.
Another country altogether.

A notice on the boat advising visitors that the Western Isles Council had
adopted a policy of Gaelic place names on road signs emphasised the foreign-ness of
the land we were approaching even more.

Winter was coming. A large lorry stacked with bales of hay from the Lowlands came off the boat at Tarbert. There is little arable land on Harris and what crop there is, this harvest, was drying in an assortment of racks, stooks and fences. Their ingenuity betrayed a desperate attempt to salvage some winter feed after the weeks of unrelenting rain.

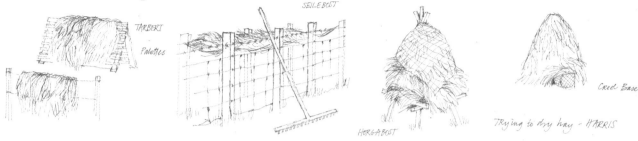

I had learned by now not to make for the furthest bolthole on arriving on an island. Boat arrival time is hang-about-and-look time.

Tarbert is the commercial capital of Harris and has an assortment of shops from the down to earth Co-Chommun store with pick axes and sheep dip to the bijoux mantelpiece ornaments and toothbrushes and black body stockings of Abdul's Drapery.

Ninety-six year old Duncan MacAskill's is further along the road. The broad wooden counters, with galvanised buckets at one end, Cadbury's milk flake at the other and wooden pigeon-hole shelves behind, were sparsely yet essentially stocked. Mr MacAskill looks smaller than he really is. He was licensed to sell tobacco until he gave up smoking two years ago. He no longer stocks cigarettes. 'Can't have temptation about'. Such resolve at ninety six!

Westwards from Tarbert the road will take you through 'fishin' and shootin' country. How infuriating it must be to have a council road go directly past the dining room window of your castle — Amhuinnsuidhe. Just opposite the now deserted, save holiday housed, island of Scarp, I met my first wild mink. Chocolate-black and furry, he inquisitively played beady eyed peep-bo in and out of the foreshore rocks as I froze in delight for twenty minutes. An escapee from intensive farming, I wished him luck. Hearach crofters would not be joining in with my sentiments.

My base in Harris was in the Northton sand dunes, overlooking the Sound of Harris. I would be going through the Sound in the Army supply ship to St Kilda in ten days time. The journey would take nine hours. I prayed for good weather.

The days on Harris got stormier and stormier.

My worst night in the van was at Northton. The roof had to be lowered in the middle of the night in a force nine. I was unable to start the van to move it to a more sheltered spot. Salt spray from the churning Sound of Harris had seeped into the engine. The incessant roar of the wind and sea, the violent rocking of the van and the never ending blackness of the night were evil and scary.

Gisbon and Rodina in the neighbouring croft insisted on inviting me in for fried herrings in oatmeal for breakfast the next day.

To celebrate my survival further with creature comforts, I dined in style that night. The van was parked in a secure hollow, backed to the still raging Sound and facing northwards to the calmer stretches of Luskentyre sands.

MAIRI'S VAN MENU
Lightly poached Raasay Chanterelles
in Orange Sauce on toast
~

Olive oil sautéed Aubergine, slow stewed in red wine,
with Waternish mint & Glendale potatoes
~

Waternish Hydroponic Cherry Tomatoes
Northton Cos Lettuce
~

Colonsay Honey dip

The guests in Scarista House, just opposite, could not have dined better, even though they had more elbow room.

The moonscape road over to Finsby prepared me for the sad dereliction of Rodel Hotel, sadder with the death of a local on his way home from the pub the previous night. Medieval Rodel church, high above it all, was a sanctuary of spacious simplicity and the finest of delicate stone carvings.

In between the wars the poor land of Harris could not support the population and a Government scheme encouraged Hearachs to move to Portnalong on Skye, where they continued their traditional lifestyle as crofter weavers. Allan MacLeod was one of the earliest of those colonisers. His daughter Joan MacDonald is now

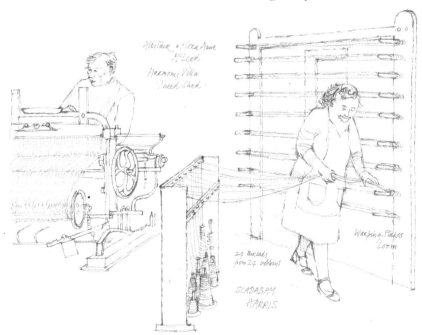

The Hills of Harris from
Northton Sand dunes

Post Mistress at Portnalong. When I was there she was relearning weaving in her mother's loom shed beside the Post Office. 'My cousin sends wool over from Harris. Go and see her.'

And so I did, finding Flora Ann and Alistair MacLeod at Scadabay. The whole process, from off the sheep's back onto the country gent's back, bar the spinning which is done in Lewis, is carried out by this warping and weaving duo. They laughed and laughed at my drawing of Cousin Joan in Skye. 'Isn't it like her?' I asked, worried. 'Yes! Yes!' they chortled.

On the way to Kyles Scalpay there is a layby and a footpath sign pointing up into the mountains saying Rhenigidale. The days of being the most isolated community in Britain with only a four mile track or sea access are numbered. The road is coming at last. After a few stops and starts. The last funding hold up stopped work only a few miles short of the village for nearly a year. Now the men and machines are in sight again.

The footpath from Kyles Scalpay is no ramblers' track. The breathtaking 'Zig-Zags' that drop from 800 feet to sea level and back up again before finally descending into the village, demand a donkey or Tibetan yak, at least.

Amazingly, three traditional houses, immaculately rendered, double glazed, re-roofed and mains electrified, stand out amidst the ruins of those deserted. One of the several Outer Isles Gatliff Trust bothies, completes the township. The newly-done up houses are smart and ready for the new road.

Waking the next morning under the tin roof of the bothy I could hear the diggers already at work high up on the hill behind.

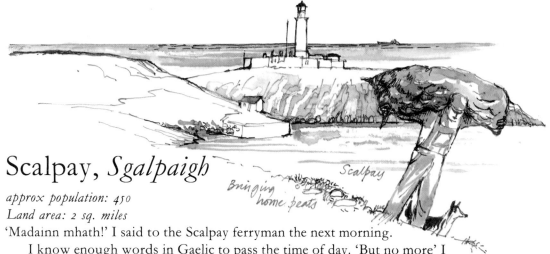

Bringing home peats

Scalpay

Scalpay, *Sgalpaigh*

approx population: 450
Land area: 2 sq. miles

'Madainn mhath!' I said to the Scalpay ferryman the next morning.

I know enough words in Gaelic to pass the time of day. 'But no more' I protested, as he responded with elaboration in his native tongue. 'I've *tried* to learn; but it is a very *difficult* language.'

'Aye,' he replied, 'I found English very difficult to learn. But I had no choice.'

Scalpay is one of the most densely populated and double-glazed smaller islands in the Western Isles. Houses nook and crannie along the shore edge; cheek by jowl over steep rocky hillsides. Unfenced potato patches, on beds raised with aeons of seaweed fertiliser, fight with the rocks for space. The sheep are fenced away on the rough interior of the island where the shallow peat banks lie.

Scalpay is a fishing island. The men away all week; the women at home knitting and cleaning those windows.

At the other end of this craggy jumbly island is Eilean Glas Lighthouse, commissioned in 1789. Today, the light is automatic and also beams another kind of message. I reached the dramatic landmark by a twenty minute bog track marked by red and white slalom poles stuck in the sludge. Outside the cavernous white-washed engine house there stood a Kenco coffee sign flapping in the wind. I had found the only 'incomers' on Scalpay, barring the Stornoway girls that have married locally. Despite the bog, accommodation is fully booked for the following season.

A Loganair plane flew very low and stylishly overhead. 'Oh—that's Dougie' (Peter? Fred? I can't remember which) 'signalling that he's on for going sailing this weekend' said the expansive owner of Eilean Glas Lighthouse.

On the way back a giant of a man browed the hill. A nineteenth century ghost carrying a woolsackful of peat back to his twentieth century Baxi-fire with Fifestone surround and teak mantelshelf.

'Feasgar math!'

I then asked him in English what the weather would do. St Kilda was next.

'*Gle dhona*. Very bad.'

St Kilda, *Hiort, September 3*

approx population: 46
Land area: 3.25 sq. miles

The Army had offered me six hours landing time on St Kilda whilst the supply ship off-loaded stores and equipment—or two and a half weeks. Nine hours in an enlarged tank landing craft merited more than six hours dry land time. For recovery, if nothing else.

Arrangements had been made for me to billet with the young National Trust wardens in the Factor's House. Being a woman I could not possibly be accommodated at the Army base.

But being a woman had major travel compensations. I was classed as 'officer material' and was elevated to the bridge and an officer's cabin, the gentleman in question having moved out, of course. Lesser civilian mortals—i.e. males—were stowed down below in the bowels of the ship.

'It'll be rough, madam,' said the young steward, offering Stugeron. I succumbed. Homeopathic travel pills, pressure point wrist bands, brandy, apple and brown bread. I took them all. And a large breakfast. They worked. Like a dream.

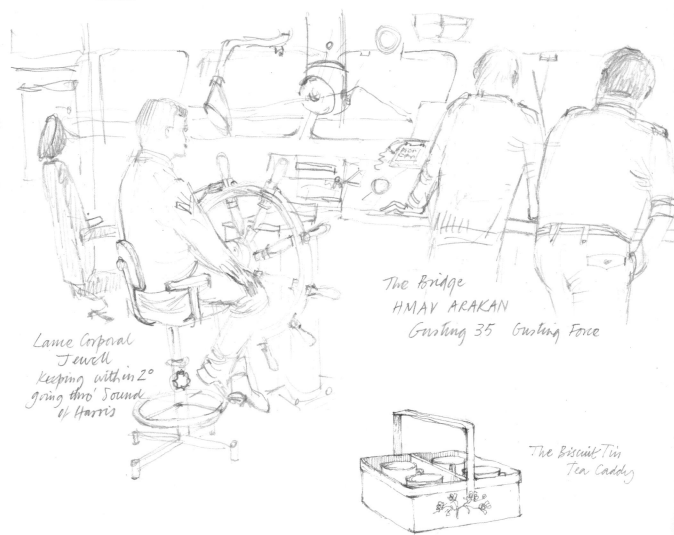

Lance Corporal
Jewell
keeping within 2°
going thro' Sound
of Harris

The Bridge
HMAV ARAKAN
Gusting 35 Gusting Force

The Biscuit Tin
Tea Caddy

IVOR
Na-h-Eagau.

Ivan, the Coastguard
showing Ozzie the Seargeant
how to check his gear before
going over the 600ft. drop of

Up on the bridge was like watching a re-run of every World War Two Navy film. The *Arakan* shimmied her way through the marker buoys in the frothing Sound of Harris. Absolute hush; two degree leeway. Asdic pinged. Terse commands issued forth from the Captain.

Then hours of shuddering, lurching and wallowing into the Atlantic Ocean. The keel of the ship juddered down and staggered up from painful impact with the relentless cross-waves.

And still further hour upon hour of clown-staggering mobility once the group of islands that make up St Kilda were discernable on the horizon line. Slowly they came nearer. Proudly majestic and indifferent to the corkscrewing little tub. Hirta, the main island flanked by the dragon's back of Dun; Soay hidden behind; Boreray and the Stacks five miles distant, like fossilized icebergs.

ARAKAN approaching
ST. KILDA . 15'00 HRS
SEPT . 3.

Mail Maybe coming in ....

St. Kilda. March Past. Sept. 12th

It was getting dusk as we came into Village Bay on Hirta. The jagged black silhouette of Dun was like a stage flat in front of the creamy gold back drop of a storm spent sky.

St Kilda makes its own weather. From hour to hour the full gamut of climatic change can be experienced. Whatever the weather the activities of man seem Lilliputian and on occasion quite ludicrous.

As well as basic supplies, Her Majesty's Army Vehicle *Arakan* was bringing boulders and gravel to St Kilda.

The Nature Conservancy Council, who lease the island from the National Trust, in turn lease sections of land to the Army. Regulations stipulate that nothing must be moved or changed. St Kilda is registered as a World Heritage Site. The sea wall by the old harbour was in need of repair; the environs of the new radar station needed to be landscaped. Hence the boulders in large skips and trailers of poly-bagged gravel now being towed by tractors down the bow ramp of the *Arakan* onto the beach.

The noise of the winches, clanging chains and powerful engines bombarded the dignity of the ancient landscape.

The
Feather Stone

SOAY & the Cambir
from below Mullach Bi.
HIRTA

Jerry drying out
one of 3 fledgling Leitch's Petrel
found drenched by generator shed.
Night flyers so possibly attracted by
burning boiler lights. Carn Mor their
nursery. Similar exercise with puffin
fledglings.

Grey Seals Jacussi
Calm Day
The Tunnel
Glen Bay
Boreray beyond

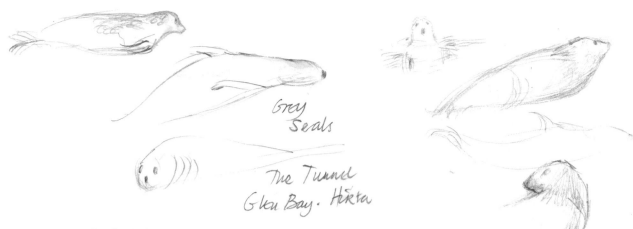

Grey
Seals

The Tunnel
Glen Bay. Hirta

Set back from the shoreline stood the watchful dwelling houses of the original
islanders; from Stone Age to late nineteenth century, shadowy in the failing light.
Hundreds of storage cleits, like memorial cairns, climbed up the dim bowl of hills
now filling with shredded cloud. Eerie in the dusk, they stood like sentinels to the
souls of the rightful owners of St Kilda.

What would they think of St Kilda now?

Soay sheep with multi-coloured eartags and research bums sprayed red and
green grazed in and around the ugly sprawl of the Army buildings. Each morning
young scientists with patient telescopes waited to collect the right shit from the
right bums. To be stored in thermoses in the deep freeze—with the kittiwake and
the catering packs of broccolli.

The Puff Inn, the squaddies' recreation centre and pub, is open to the civilian
fray of contractors, scientists, NCC and NT, yachties—and this 'civvie drawrer'.
An Acapulco dive from the top of the bar is the initiation test for braver idiots
than I.

The St Kildans would have paid great attention to the Coastguard Rescue
practice. 'We work from the top down, the Mountain Rescue from the bottom
up,' said Ivan the Coastguard from Harris, to Ozzie the Sergeant from Geordieland,
as the latter was lowered over the 600 foot cliff at Na-h-Eagan in a brightly coloured
canvas nappie.

And what would they think about the once fortnightly film shows? (Pinnochio
is as rousingly violent as Rambo to some squaddies.) To say nothing of the
television videos and scientific gadgetry that the continuously humming generators
maintain.

The stones around Village Bay stay silent.

If you go over to the other side of the island to Gleann Mor, the unadulterated
St Kilda swallows you up in a time warp of further silence. The ancient stone-built
'horned' structures, so called from the semi-circular forecourts, are unique to
Europe. Possibly dating from the sixth century, they evolved in isolation. Recent
generations of St Kildans used them, unchanged, for summer shielings. Some still
have their turf roofs.

It was a low cloud day. Boreray and the Stacks were swathed in tendrils of
vapour. Round about me spirits weaved in the mist. A great skua with precise and
mute malevolence nearly scalped my head. Further on towards Soay on the Cambir,
truly wild Soay sheep, unlike Nellie and her lamb at the back door of the cookhouse,
bounded over and down sheer cliff faces.

Dun
Ungrazed since '30s —
like walking on a
trampoline

Jerry & Jo, the fulmars,
the hog weed & the wren.

It was too late in the year to see the puffins but I had the rare opportunity of going over with Jo and Gerry, the National Trust wardens, in the Army inflatable to Dun. They wanted to collect fungi and check on the colony's deserted burrows. Reports from Shetland had indicated a high fledgling mortality this year. As it turned out, the fledgling puffins of Dun had safely migrated.

The day was sunny and magical. Dun has been ungrazed since 1930. We slithered and slipped through the primeval growth of mayweed and sorrel which treacherously hid the burrows—and guano. Fulmars, ever watchful, silently glided by. Out at the rocky bare ocean-carved headland I heard the ultimate St Kilda contradiction—the sweet country garden song of a wren. To the west, over the glittering sea, America, the nearest landfall.

Leaving St Kilda at 1.00 a.m. of a stormy black night I threw a message in a bottle over the side of HMAV *Arakan*. I know someone will find it one day.

cheaper to fly to Majorca etc.

Tunsgarry
& Uig Sands.
W. LEWIS.

Lewis, *Leodhas, September 25*

approx population: 21,413
Land area: 680 sq. miles

What a sense of deflation I experienced on returning to the mainland of the Uists after St Kilda. Only the skies were redeeming.

I was instantly struck by the row upon row of fences so stark and regimented on the flat land of Benbecula. Miles of little sticks dividing up the landscape into squares. Suddenly I realised that fish farming cages were the inevitable extension to man's age old need to compartmentalise and control his environment. Fish cages are no more of an eyesore than fences. We are just not used to the surface of lochs being divided up into sections—yet. The landscape has been, for long enough.

There was no time for maudlin memories of the wilderness days of St Kilda. I had to get to Lewis as quickly as possible via Lochmaddy in North Uist and Tarbert, in Harris. Though only the end of September, the nights were drawing in. There is no cushioned Autumn in the Outer Isles. Winter comes directly and unsympathetically with monotonous winds that are known to cause madness.

The van did not seem to like my return, despite nearly three weeks break from each other. She responded very reluctantly to any pressure to speed us on our way north. I recognised the symptoms. Sheer exhaustion.

The island of Lewis and Harris is the third biggest land mass in Britain after Ireland. Over twenty-one and a half thousand people live in Lewis; the northernmost end being the most densely populated rural area in Europe. A high mountain range separates the two 'islands'. Coming down the Lewis side the sloping moors are afforested. Further on, to disprove the common myth that no trees grow in the Outer Hebrides, the township of Ballalan has many a fine mature sycamore and ever hardy willows. No autumn leaves, however. The wind blows them off before they have time to change colour.

The Pairc district, to the east, is definitely treeless. Rocky and barren, it is surely uninhabited? Great road widening excavations were making their way to where-on-earth? Pairc and South Lochs are fish farming country. At Lemreway, in wind whipped drizzle, men in yellow oilskins mended fish cage nets hanging from high poles.

One would not dare to question the morality of fish-farming in these parts. Hundreds of people are employed in expanding the economy—and road. But is there not surely something wrong with a society that can so insensitively cage animals, birds and fish for commercial gain? Most insensitive of all is the pump ashore system where maturing salmon are forced to continuously swim round and round in one direction only against an artificial current for all of their limited lives. Perhaps a Society for the Prevention of Cruelty to Fish needs to be formed.

A travelling van stopped by the workmen for cigarette sales and gossip. Twenty-two-year old Sheena travels from her home in the picturesque fjord of Gravir six days a week and covers 300 miles, a lifeline to many of the elderly people who live in the area. 'You're "for it" if you are late; you're "for it" if you are *early*!' Sheena smiled. She is so slim she can have the widest of shelves jam-packed with groceries and goods on each side of the inside of the van.

Over to the west the day was clearing. Not a car or van passed either way. The empty curving sands of Uig wound inward under the shadow of purple hills. The clouds had lifted. From the top of Mealsival I willed to see St Kilda far beyond the visible Flannan Isles.

Bernera provided a substitute St Kilda for my nostalgic eye to savour. On the Atlantic side is a group of islands collectively called Little Bernera. Fast-moving clouds staged a *chiaroscuro* dance over cliffs and stacks, the endless sea stretching behind.

The van was seriously rebelling the further north we travelled. Passing the sixty-six—I counted them—wooden summer shieling huts on the moors behind Stornoway, some still gaily painted and with lace curtains, I wished I could squat in the prettiest one until the project was over. The van must have taken note. My wish came true. Not exactly as imagined but strangely accurate in reality.

The van broke down finally and irretrievably—with only a week left of 'The Journey' to do. She had had enough. Her innards had packed in completely.

Stornoway with all its wide-ranging urban facilities was more welcome than I would normally have admitted. I hired a cheap red car, feeling like a failing third rate travelling salesman wondering where the next bed would be.

As it turned out, a most generous friend of a friend on hearing of the downward spiral of my ignominious finale offered her temporarily empty cottage in Skigersta in Ness. Just where I had been heading for . . .

The synchronicity continued. Fighting my way round the gale-swept Butt of Lewis lighthouse, grateful for four thick walls and a peat fire a-waiting me at the end of the day, I met up with Calum MacKay, one of the relief lighthouse keepers. And one of the 'Ten Men of Ness'. His home was opposite the house I had been loaned. That island hospitality took over again and I was fed and watered and regaled with tales of the Guga Hunt.

Everyone knows at length about the St Kilda inhabitants' death defying harvesting of the gannets or gugas, off the sheer cliffs of Borreray, Stac an Armin and Stac Lee, five miles distant from Hirta. But few realise that such skills were the natural order of the late summer for the men of Ness on Lewis as well, who not only went to the nearest gannetry on Sula Sgeir but to North Rona and St Kilda, a hundred miles west, *rowing* all the way.

The people of Ness kept the tradition in Sula Sgeir going long after the first fish fingers came to the deep freezes of the northernmost island of the Hebrides. Conservationists have fought hard to end 'this barbaric ancient ritual'. The way